Brimming with creative inspiration, how-to projects, and useful information to enrich your everyday life, Quarto Knows is a favourite destination for those pursuing their interests and passions. Visit our site and dig deeper with our books into your area of interest: Quarto Creates, Quarto Cooks, Quarto Homes, Quarto Lives, Quarto Drives, Quarto Explores, Quarto Gifts, or Quarto Kids.

First published in 2017 by Voyageur Press, an imprint of The Quarto Group,
401 Second Avenue North, Suite 310, Minneapolis, MN 55401 USA.
T: (612) 344-8100 F: (612) 344-8692   QuartoKnows.com

Voyageur Press titles are also available at discount for retail, wholesale, promotional, and bulk purchase. For details, contact the Special Sales Manager by email at specialsales@quarto.com or by mail at The Quarto Group, Attn: Special Sales Manager, 401 Second Avenue North, Suite 310, Minneapolis, MN 55401 USA.

10 9 8 7 6 5 4 3 2

ISBN: 978-0-7603-5261-8

Library of Congress Cataloging-in-Publication Data

Names: Janzen, Emma, 1986- author.
Title: Mezcal : the history, craft & cocktails of the world's ultimate
   artisanal spirit / Emma Janzen.
Description: Minneapolis, MN, USA : Voyageur Press, 2017. | Includes
   bibliographical references and index.
Identifiers: LCCN 2017004250 | ISBN 9780760352618 (hardback)
Subjects: LCSH: Mescal. | Cocktails. | BISAC: COOKING / Beverages / Wine &
   Spirits. | HISTORY / Latin America / Mexico. | LCGFT: Cookbooks.
Classification: LCC TP607.M46 J36 2017 | DDC 641.2/5--dc23
LC record available at https://lccn.loc.gov/2017004250

Acquiring Editor: Dennis Pernu
Project Manager: Madeleine Vasaly
Art Director: James Kegley
Cover & Page Designer: Studio Mpls
Layout: Ashley Prine, Tandem Books

Page 1: One of the most common drinking vessels for mezcal is the *veladora*, basically an upcycled candleholder. Because each glass bears a cross on the bottom, there's a saying in mezcal country that goes, *Hasta que ver a la cruz*—"Drink until you see the cross."
Page 2–3: Agave piñas await roasting. *Jose de Jesus Churion Del/Shutterstock*

Printed in China

MIX
Paper from
responsible sources
FSC® C101537

MEZCAL

THE HISTORY, CRAFT & COCKTAILS OF THE
WORLD'S ULTIMATE ARTISANAL SPIRIT

EMMA JANZEN

VOYAGEUR
PRESS

CONTENTS

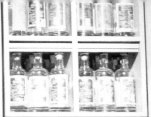

AN INTRODUCTION

MEZCAL IS THE MOST COMPLEX SPIRIT IN THE WORLD.

I know; it sounds trite. It's oversimplified. It's lacking a certain panache that many others will spout when talking about mezcal. But it's always the first refrain on everyone's lips—an incantation that's been repeated to me so frequently throughout the years I've spent getting to know the spirit that it's firmly tattooed in my consciousness. Now that I'm deeply invested, I can't imagine a better way to describe it.

Everything about Mexico's indigenous spirit—from the biological diversity of the raw material that goes into it to the tiny differences in the way the liquor is produced by different distillers and the expressive flavors that emerge as a result—will stop the average spirits lover in their tracks with its mind-boggling level of sheer nuance and *complexity*.

Maybe you've heard mezcal described as bottom-shelf "rotgut," as people like to say. Maybe you know it as "tequila's mysterious, smoky cousin," a phrase I admit to regurgitating in my first article on the spirit published back in 2010. I'd like to put a stop to both frames of reference. Yes, mezcal often has a smoky element to its flavor. Yes, in the last fifty years or so, the mezcal industry has been dominated by mass-produced swill, so it's easy to find liquid made with god knows what added to the distillate and decorated with a deceased red agave worm. But this kind of mezcal is not the delicious and culturally rich spirit that's been simmering under the surface throughout Mexico for centuries. It's not the mezcal that we're seeing crawl back into the light today.

So let's forget about the mezcal with the poor reputation for now and open our minds to its predecessor: a spirit with a rich cultural heritage and absolutely stunning flavor that's unmatched in the world of distillation.

It's easy to wax poetic about it because the agave spirit has a captivating and storied history. It has weaved through the fabric of Mexican culture for centuries, with some scientists dating evidence of first distillation to Mesoamerican times. It's rustic, humble, brazen, fiery, and romantic all at the same time. Historically, special mezcals have been made to celebrate the births of children, offered to sanctify marriages, and poured to commemorate the dead at funerals. In some communities, it has been used as medicine, to heal the body and the soul. In others, it has been consumed ritualistically, to symbolize fertility and encourage the return of each rainy season to ensure a blessed crop to come.

So how did we get to the crappy bottle with the worm? As indigenous communities evolved and modernized, the spirit's relevance and ritual diminished. In an *Artes de México* essay titled "Of Wisdom and Eternity," poet Fausto Rasero writes: "Banned during colonial times for its connection to pagan festivals and its interference with brandy and wine imports from Spain, mezcal was only recently able to shed the stigma of its illicit, humble origins." The old ways of production weren't totally wiped out, though—and that's key to our story today. The small-format, community-centric model has survived the whole time; it's just been operating on the fringes of our agave consciousness. Now the small, traditional outfits are finding their day in the sun again, and here in America, we're starting to see an increase in great quality mezcals.

In the larger scheme of global spirits, mezcal is still a speck on the map. In 2015, only 2.4 million liters were produced, compared with tequila's 228.5 million. The spirit only captures 0.03 percent of the global market. But its growth is impressive; production more than doubled from 2011 to 2016, and as of 2015, producers were shipping cases to forty-eight countries around the world. The trajectory will only keep growing from here.

Because cultural heritage is at stake, it's important to keep tabs on which producers are making mezcal in an honorable fashion and which ones are out to make a quick buck as the category stretches (more on this later). It's also important to keep in mind that the spirit's mysticism isn't the only thing at stake moving forward. The recent resurgence of artisanal and traditional mezcal also represents a piece of the puzzle that's helping Mexico's economy grow.

When I was in Oaxaca in 2016, I traveled to several of the Mezcal Vago *palenques*, or distilleries, located in remote regions of the state. I first wrote about Vago when the company launched in the States back in 2013, and the heart-warming backstory has stuck with me since, so I wanted to visit the

MEZCAL SALES IN THE UNITED STATES GREW BY NEARLY 48 PERCENT BETWEEN 2007 AND 2011, AND EXPLODED FROM A $10 MILLION INDUSTRY IN 2005 TO $126 MILLION IN 2015.

source and see where the magic happens. In its most simplified version, the narrative of the brand goes like this: Judah Kuper, Colorado surf and ski bum, is traveling around the Mexican coast and lands in the hospital with an earache. There, he meets the woman of his dreams, the lovely Valentina, who happens to come from a family that makes mezcal. The two end up marrying, and Judah decides to export the mezcal to America. Why not share the beautiful liquid and rich culture of his adopted family with his compatriots? Now, thanks to the success of the business, many members of Valentina's family make mezcal full-time, as a primary source of income.

On the speed-bump-riddled road from Oaxaca City to Sola de Vega, Mezcal Vago brand and operations manager Francisco Terrazas asked me what kinds of questions I wanted him to translate for maestro Salomón Rey Rodriguez during our visit. I said I was interested in his philosophy. Why make mezcal? Many producers have said now is the time to get in the game before the industry overcrowds. Others ramble on about the spirituality and romanticism. They spout the myth of Mayahuel and her four hundred rabbits.

Terrazas says that for Tío Rey, the spirituality isn't necessarily in the mezcal itself, but rather in the fact that he gets to make the spirit for a living. That's the blessing: the act of making it. "I'm not trying to shit on any romantic ideal of mezcal," he explained, "but to really get it, I think you have to realize the pragmatic reality and combine that with your appreciation of the spirit. That's truly the only way to understand where mezcal is right now."

That notion of balance stayed with me throughout the course of writing this book. Mezcal is spiritual and cultural and historic, but at the end of the day it's important because the profits put food on the table. Some of these producers don't own closed-toed shoes. Others barely have a roof over their heads. Demand means new jobs; it's why natives are able to stay in their country instead of leaving to find work in the States and why many immigrants are moving back to Mexico to carry on the traditions of their people. The blessing isn't always the mezcal itself, but the act of making it.

A few notes about my approach. First, mezcal, whether it can be legally called as such or not, is made all over Mexico, and within each state and region, traditions and production secrets differ. So when it comes to talking about what mezcal *is*—the history, techniques, flavors—speaking in absolutes simply doesn't work. You can't say mezcal from Guerrero will taste similar to one made in Puebla, because mezcal is wild and free and (almost totally) unrestricted in how one can approach the production details. For this reason, in the pages that follow you'll find a sprinkling of perspectives from other regions and producers to paint a more complete picture of what the spirit embodies. But 95 percent of mezcal exports are still centered in Oaxaca today, so the text is largely representative of that area. In other words, don't view this as a dogmatic, absolute "this is mezcal in its entirety" kind of guide. Rather, look at it as a snapshot of where things stand today.

As agave expert Iván Saldaña Oyarzábal writes in *The Anatomy of Mezcal,* "Mezcal should make us humble. There are dimensions of mezcal that cannot be grasped using rational information, history or biology. Perhaps it is the overall sensory experience that it creates, the state of the mind and the emotions it can bring on. The shamans of the Zapotec and the Mixe regions use it to travel and think."

I wholeheartedly agree with this. Knowing mezcal is not simply grasping the difference between a *karwinskii* and an *angustifolia*. It's not about understanding the ins and outs of fermentation and distillation. It's a time and a place and a memory, and in a more cerebral sense, it's knowing that you'll never know every little detail about the spirit and being totally OK with that—a sentiment that's been delivered to me time and time again by producers, brand representatives, and wise bartenders.

Enjoy the journey of getting to know mezcal, and don't forget it's a gift made for us to enjoy here, now, when we have some of the best quality expressions at our fingertips. The nuts and bolts outlined in the following pages are simply building blocks to starting down the road of understanding. From there, it's about developing your own relationship with the liquid.

Salud!

PART ONE

MEETING MAYAHUEL

In traditional mezcal, every batch is unique and unrepeatable when it comes to flavors and aromas. . . . The only way to learn more about mezcal is to try everything.

—Silvia Philion, Mezcaloteca

The streets of Oaxaca City feel serene at 5:00 p.m. on a Tuesday evening, so it's unsurprising that my husband and I are the only ones with reservations for a mezcal tasting at Mezcaloteca. The seven-year-old *mezcaleria* is run by Silvia Philion and partner Marco Ochoa, who arrive with a rambunctious toddler in tow. As they get settled, we take the opportunity to soak up the reverent atmosphere. With a bookshelf-like back bar and educational literature set up at every station, the name rings true: Mezcaloteca feels more like a cozy library than a bar, and as we quickly discover, Philion makes for the perfect mezcal historian.

"Getting to know mezcal is tricky," Philion says as she pulls up a stool on the other side of the bar. "When I first tried it I liked it, but for many people it's something you have to learn to like. It's like the first time you try beer—nobody likes it at first."

She's a wellspring of knowledge and a soulful teacher who speaks with a studied confidence and an infectious passion. To start, she shares the bar's backstory: The couple comes from a long line of mezcal producers, and once they caught the spark for the spirit, they migrated from Mexico City to Oaxaca

opposite: Mezcaloteca co-owner Silvia Philion is a wealth of knowledge on mezcal. Her Oaxacan mezcaleria is one of the best in the world.

Oaxaca to run the family ranch (they also manage Mezcalosfera, a brand currently exported to the States). "We were traveling back and forth to the city, and always wondered why there was not a place in Oaxaca where you can get educated on mezcal: how it's made, the different regions, different flavors and aromas, diversity of plants, et cetera," Philion explains. "That's why we created Mezcaloteca—a place where people can learn about maestro *mezcaleros* and their traditional way of producing."

Most Mezcaloteca visitors· have the basics down already, she says. Enthusiasts understand mezcal is a distilled spirit that can be made only in Mexico. It's created with the heart of the agave plant (also known as a *maguey* in Spanish). With roots that trace back centuries, mezcal was named for the Nahuatl term for cooked agave, because unlike tequila, the agave plants must be roasted before they can be transformed into mezcal.

At the bar, the education continues. A poster-sized map identifies the sizes, shapes, and personalities of the approximately

Mezcaloteca in Oaxaca opened with the goal of educating people about mezcal and its history.

MEZCAL VS. TEQUILA

Tequila is simply the legal name for one type of mezcal. Mezcal can be produced from up to fifty different species of the agave plant, including the one that tequila must be made from: *Agave tequilana weber*. For this reason, the flavors in tequila can be far less varied between brands than those in mezcal. Tequila is also usually steamed in ovens instead of roasted underground, so the definitive smoke characteristic is often absent. Finally, like mezcal, tequila has a regulated Appellation of Origin (Denominación de Origen, or DO) and can only be made in the states of Jalisco, Guanajuato, Tamaulipas, Nayarit, and Michoacán.

fifty species of maguey that can be used to make mezcal, which plants grow where, and how they reproduce. A pamphlet explains traditional mezcal must be 100 percent agave, and the alcohol content should typically land around 45 percent. Facts and figures etched on a chalkboard lay out the spirit's formal geographic boundaries, and each bottle is marked with a laundry list of production stats to further the lessons. As I study the material, Philion slides over a few *veladoras*, sipping glasses popular for serving mezcal, and asks where we want to start our journey.

Newcomers would likely begin with an *espadín*, the friendliest introduction to the spirit and the most commonly distilled agave varietal on the market right now, but since this isn't my first rodeo, I ask for one of Philion's current favorites. A thirty-year-old *tepeztate* made by a young mezcalero from Oaxaca appears in the glass. A sense memory from my childhood hits immediately: warm, umami-rich grilled cheese with a flavor of buttered toast, plus bright banana notes and heaps of cinnamon—like the woody, autumnal broomsticks you can buy at the grocery store in the fall. It's deep, muscular, and herbal, "but like old herbs," she adds. "Really old, wise herbs."

Many a maestro has exclaimed, "mezcal tastes like time," because the plants take so long to mature and the production process is slow and laborious. Patience is key to making good mezcal. Depending on the species and variety, agaves take anywhere from five to thirty-five years to reach maturity, making for extremely expressive flavors. And while formal connections between where the plant was grown and its expression of *terroir* in the glass haven't been established, many agree it's an exciting notion to explore.

opposite: The walls and shelves at Philion's Mezcaloteca are like a library, lined with educational materials and knickknacks.

above: Every station at the bar at Mezcaloteca is equipped with a map of agave varieties and a guide to identifying good mezcal.

opposite: A hollowed-out gourd, or *jícara*, is a traditional vessel used to serve mezcal.

For our next round, Philion wanted to give us a taste of this concept, so we try two kinds of mezcals made from *Agave cupreata*: a 2011 *papalome* (the regional slang for *cupreata*) from a small producer in Puebla, and a 2014 *papalote* from the Sanzekan co-op in the state of Guerrero. The former tastes bone dry with hints of grassy herbs, while the latter lands on the brighter end of the spectrum with pretty, floral characteristics like white lilies and honey. Though they're made from the same species, their personalities couldn't be more different.

At this point, you might wonder why I haven't mentioned smoke yet. Mezcal's signature characteristic is without a doubt its smoky flavor, which is a byproduct of the production process. Unlike tequila, which is cooked with steam, mezcal is produced when the hearts, or *piñas*, of the agave plant are slowly roasted over burning coals and wood, usually in an underground pit. The smoky attribute is what most drinkers notice at first, but a wide breadth of flavors extends far beyond that veil of smoke. From earthy and dusty to verdant and herbaceous, the spirit's many personalities are as beautiful and diverse as all of the styles of craft beer or the spices used in Indian cuisine. No two mezcals taste exactly the same.

Old distillation tools sit in a corner at Mezcaloteca.

This diversity comes from everywhere—from the plants themselves, from where they are grown, from how long it takes them to reach maturity, from how and when they are harvested, and from how the maestro mezcalero (the distiller) carries out each step of production. Every choice influences the flavor of the mezcal. "With traditional mezcal," Philion emphasizes, "every batch is unique and unrepeatable when it comes to flavors and aromas." The region of Mexico where the mezcal is produced also matters.

Philion points to the chalkboard map on the wall behind the bar that breaks down the spirit's formal Appellation of Origin (Denominación de Origen) for the spirit. For centuries the term *mezcal* was used to describe every batch of liquor made from agave plants regardless of where or how it was made. Then, in 1994, the Mexican government created the first round of formal geographic restrictions. The regulations are controversial for many reasons (one of which is the high cost to become certified, which has put the

Mezcaloteca was one of the first mezcal producers to insist on including detailed production information on bottle labels. The more transparency, the easier it is to understand the flavors inside, Silvia Philion says.

above: One of the best ways to learn about mezcal is by trying as many as you can.

right: Mezcal's Appellation of Origin, or Denominación de Origen, is one of the largest in the world, with nine of Mexico's thirty-one states included. This system determines which states' agave spirits may be labeled as mezcal.

process out of reach for many generations-old producers), but today the liquid can only be called mezcal if produced in nine of Mexico's thirty-one states: Oaxaca, Durango, Zacatecas, San Luis Potosí, Guanajuato, Guerrero, Tamaulipas, Michoacán, and Puebla. Like Champagne or Cognac, if it's made outside of these regulated states, it must be called something else, like *bacanora* (made only in Sonora) or *raicilla* (a term that's not yet legally regulated, but made in Jalisco, nevertheless).

Of the large territory where mezcal can be called as such, Oaxaca currently has the highest concentration of producers; in 2015, 422 were recorded by the CRM (the regulatory committee

EACH MEZCAL FROM DIFFERENT REGIONS IN MEXICO REPRESENTS THE CULTURE WHERE THEY ARE PRODUCED. IT'S LIKE TRADITIONAL CLOTHING; THERE IS A LOT OF DIFFERENT INDIGENOUS CLOTHING AROUND MEXICO, AND IT'S NOT LIKE ONE IS BETTER THAN THE OTHER ONE–THEY ARE DIFFERENT AND REPRESENT DIFFERENT BACKGROUNDS AND IDENTITIES. HAVING A SIP OF EACH MEZCAL PRODUCED IN DIFFERENT REGIONS IS LIKE GETTING TO KNOW EACH COMMUNITY.

–PEDRO JIMÉNEZ, PARE DE SUFRIR

for mezcal in Mexico), compared to 79 in Guerrero, 23 in Michoacán, and 19 in Durango. Because Oaxaca is where a lot of the products first emerged, about 95 percent of the mezcal exported out of Mexico today comes from that state. But as production grows in other areas, releases from Michoacán, Guerrero, and Puebla are starting to trickle over the border. That trickle should only grow in the coming years. "Oaxaca is the most emblematic state because of its diversity, but you can find very good mezcal in all of Mexico," Philion says. "Be open to try stuff from other states, because it's all in the terroir, no? Other states will have different weather, water, soil, so that will change everything."

While other states will soon flood the market with their tapestry of unique mezcals, for our final sips of the tasting, Philion asks if we want to stay local and try something that's "very Oaxacan". She pours two varieties that are endemic to the state but totally opposing in flavors: a *tobalá* from the *potatorum* species to start and a *bicuixe* from the *Agave karwinskii* species to contrast. "*Karwinskii* is such a great surprise to every palate, because we're used to the smoky flavors of mezcal," she explains. "When you try a *karwinskii*, you realize a mezcal can also be herbal, fresh, floral." The tobalá lands near the woody, dry, and smoky end of the spectrum, with hints of leather and some lingering sweetness. The *karwinskii*? As promised: dry, but crispy in its freshness. Again, both are mezcal, but the diversity in flavor never fails to astound.

A Spanish-speaking couple pulls up a set of stools at the other end of the bar, and as the activity picks up, we drain our last drops of mezcal. Trying so many styles side by side is invaluable, but the best part of visiting Mezcaloteca is Philion's fervor for the spirit. She's one of the true evangelists, preserving the culture and history of mezcal so that as it becomes popular, people don't lose sight of the spirit's roots. I'll drink to that any day of the week.

A BRIEF MODERN HISTORY

To understand traditional mezcal's recent leap to the international stage, we begin a few decades back to get a snapshot of how things stood at the precipice of change. For this, I turned to a somewhat unlikely source—a fellow Chicagoan who has spent decades traveling to and from Mexico, soaking up the culture one bite (or in this case, sip) at a time: chef Rick Bayless.

"I first got into mezcal culture forty years ago when I was living in a small village in the state of Guerrero," the James Beard Award–winning chef and author says. At that time, production was largely centered in remote villages and everything was artisanal and ancestral—brand names didn't exist. "We went up into the mountains and harvested agave to take to the village distillery," Bayless continues. "There was one guy who was the maestro mezcalero and he would oversee production in that particular village. It was like having a bakery in town where you would take your dough to the baker and he would bake it for you. A lot of village life was like that. Families specialized in different things."

Fresh mezcal, pulled directly from the still, has a remarkably fresh flavor, even at an alcohol percentage that could tip the scale at over 100 proof. This mezcal is being served in hollowed half-gourds called *jícaras*—the most traditional vessel for drinking mezcal.

Mezcal distilleries are often family affairs going back generations. Graciela Angeles Carreño runs operations at Real Minero, where her family has been producing mezcal since the 1800s.

When Bayless moved to Oaxaca years later, the situation was similar, though some mezcal could be found in the city center. "It was rotgut stuff," he says. "Nobody I knew would drink that—they said it was just for the tourists."

One found the good stuff by word of mouth. "Everybody would say, 'So-and-so makes my mezcal in that town over there.' It was such a wonderful thing to think about just how important a part of everyday life mezcal was, not only in this village, but in every village. It was *the* beverage."

Things stayed this way in Mexico until a free-spirited artist from California named Ron Cooper lit the first sparks of change. "The Godfather" of mezcal, as he's now known, first discovered the spirit on a road trip along the Pan American Highway in the 1960s. Drawn back time and time again, he started Del Maguey to bring the captivating liquid back to America to share with

TRADITIONAL MEZCAL HAS ALWAYS BEEN FAMOUS IN THE TOWNS WHERE IT'S PRODUCED, BUT IT WAS VERY ISOLATED TO THOSE TOWNS AND COMMUNITIES. IT'S NEW FOR US, BUT NOT NEW FOR THEM.

—SILVIA PHILION,
MEZCALOTECA

MYTHS AND LEGENDS

As with many ancient spirits, mezcal has its fair share of origin stories and legends. The most common features Mayahuel, the Aztec goddess of fertility and agave who was deified in the pulque-producing area of the Central Highlands. The goddess has been depicted with four hundred breasts to feed her many children, also known as the four hundred rabbits, or gods of drunkenness. Another myth has to do with a sneaky possum, or *tlacuache*, who stole mezcal, fire, and tobacco from the demons as an offering to the gods.

above: With quality mezcal, the label will detail important production information, including the type of oven, fermentation vessel, still, and the date of distillation.

right: The artisanal nature of mezcal production is one reason for its recent rise. One of the most common tools used to crush agave is the *tahona*, a large stone wheel. A mule typically drags the system in a circular fashion.

friends. The first products—an espadín from San Luis del Rio and another from Chichicapa—were officially imported in 1995. "You don't find mezcal. Mezcal finds you," he says. "So mezcal found me, and I started Del Maguey as an art project. Up until about [2012], it stayed an art project. It has only really become a business in the last four years."

Finding a way to introduce this so-called new cultural liquid to unsuspecting Americans wasn't always easy, and Cooper met the same suspicions Bayless encountered when he toured Mexico with bottles in tow. "The good mezcal never left the villages," Cooper says, adding that people in Oaxaca City and Mexico City turned their noses up at the spirit even in the 1990s because it had a reputation for being the poor man's drink. "I went to Mexico City to the Camino Real—the most beautiful hotel I've ever seen, designed by architect Ricardo Legorreta for the Olympics in 1968—I tried convincing them to put mezcal on the cart they roll around in the bar, and nobody would have anything to do with it."

Converting one person at a time—"nose by nose," he says—ended up being his life's quest. It took a good number of years for the spirit to gain traction, but the mood eventually shifted as people with culinary backgrounds found favor in the spirit. "The first circle of people to accept Del Maguey were chefs, because they had great palates and they knew what they were tasting," Cooper says. "They didn't know about how mezcal was made or where it came from, but when they tasted it, they knew there was something really complex and incredible."

Bar industry veterans like Jimmy Yeager of Jimmy's restaurant in Aspen and Tony Abou-Ganim of the Bellagio in Las Vegas also took notice. In 1998,

Mezcal quickly found favor with the bartending crowd, who discovered the spirit works splendidly in cocktails.

Bars around the country now stock impressive collections of mezcal. This is La Condesa in Austin, Texas.

Yeager invited Cooper to participate in the *Food & Wine Classic* in Aspen. "It was this incredible international event and we're the first spirit there with a table," Cooper says, adding that Del Maguey attended for the next eighteen years. Once sommelier Steve Olsen entered the picture, Cooper says, the rest was history. "It was a Saturday night after this big Latino salsa party at Jimmy's restaurant, and Tom Colicchio and Mario Batali are there and all we do is drink tobalá and beer all night," he says. "Jimmy makes breakfast at dawn and Steve and Jimmy pull me aside, and they say, 'We've made a decision. We're never going to let Del Maguey fail.'" Cooper pauses as he reflects on the night. "I'm just this ignorant guy who's never dealt in the spirits business. I'm an artist. I drank wine, I liked beer, but I had no idea about how to promote [mezcal]."

THE RISING TIDE

Over the course of two decades, what started as a humble "art project" evolved into a force of nature, thanks to Cooper's diligent work and army of loyal converts. Chefs and bartenders continued to join the mezcal camp, and by the mid-2000s, Del Maguey seemed like an empire of single-village mezcals, paving the road for other brands to enter the market. By 2008 and 2009, brands like Sombra, Ilegal, Fidencio, and Los Amantes were filtering into the country; bartender Phil Ward left high-profile New York cocktail bar Death & Co. to open the agave-focused Mayahuel; and publications like the *New York Times* and *Saveur* began taking an interest in the spirit.

above: This mural at the Pastry War details the bar's primary rule: no agave spirits made with industrial methods!

right: The back bar at the Pastry War in Houston, Texas, carries a thoughtful selection of mezcal.

Fidencio Mezcal launched in 2009 with founder Arik Torren at the helm. The New Yorker had a background in the restaurant business, and certain cultural changes led him to believe the atmosphere was ripe for traditional mezcal. "People were changing; we were evolving into accepting things that are bitter, smoky—flavors that are dynamic and polarizing," he says. "There was also a focus on going back to the farm, and there's no spirit more on that level than mezcal. This is a real deep spirit category in a world of flash-in-the-pan ones."

That new cultural climate has only strengthened since. In 2016, *Bloomberg* reported that mezcal has started to make inroads in sales as well. "From 2010 to 2015, combined sales of tequila and mezcal rose 30 percent by volume in the US, more than any other alcohol category except Cognac," staffers wrote. By comparison, according to data from Euromonitor International, vodka sales only increased 17 percent during the same window.

Bars like Masa Azul in Chicago, Barrio in Seattle, and Las Perlas in Los Angeles, were some of the early adopters amassing stockpiles of mezcal, but in 2013, the playing field changed when bar impresarios Bobby Heugel and partner Alba Huerta opened the Pastry War in Houston. The program stocked the bar with notable bottles, and it still actively educates the public about where mezcal comes from and how it's made. The spirits menu is organized by agave type and it lists detailed information like production year, still type, and the name of the maestro mezcalero for each expression. On the wall behind the bar, a mural lists all spirits the bar will *not* serve, like mezcal brands with worms in the bottle, flavored agave spirits, and mass-produced liquid. Together with a well-educated staff, the bar put forward an advocacy for the spirit that other places wouldn't dare attempt at the time.

Subsequently, a new wave of mezcal-focused bars have opened. Espita Mezcaleria in Washington, D.C., Mezcaleria Las Flores in Chicago, and Mezcalito in San Francisco launched in 2016 with a vow to carry the torch ignited by the Pastry War. Each takes care to inform guests of the colorful history of mezcal, offering flights and cocktails as a means for introduction. The same year, having been nominated three times in a row, Ron Cooper won the James Beard Award for Outstanding Wine, Beer, or Spirits Professional. "My job now is keeper of the customs," Cooper says. "It's become very apparent to me over the course of these twenty-odd years that I'm really bringing culture—Mexican, Oaxacan, Zapotec, Mixte culture—to the world. Mezcal is a ritual beverage."

opposite: The bar at Mezcaleria Tobalá in Austin, Texas, carries a great selection of mezcal labels.

above: Two veladoras of mezcal rest on a table at El Palenquito in Mexico City.

right: El Palenquito is a Mexico City mezcal bar featuring small-batch bottles from around the country.

ACROSS THE BORDER

Cooper's success in America triggered big waves south of the border too. What was once considered dismissible swill continues to ease back into the collective consciousness. "Things changed slowly," Cooper says. "I think it was more a result of it being accepted in the United States, and then word filtering back to Mexico that it was cool to drink mezcal."

The culture continues to expand all over Mexico's larger metropolitan areas, as quality brands surface and challenge mass-produced industrial labels. Misty Kalkofen, "Madrina" at Del Maguey who worked on the bartending side of the industry before joining Cooper's flock, frequently travels to Mexico City and Oaxaca City for the

above: Alipus offers many bottles at their Mexico City mezcaleria that aren't available in the United States.

opposite: A visit to Alipus Mezcaleria in Mexico City is a must for those looking to get a feel for the work of a single brand.

company. "My first experience in Mexico City was five or six years ago, and no one was drinking mezcal," she remembers. "Especially the older crowd. They were drinking brandy, Scotch, or rum. In some cases, tequila. I recently did a huge trade show and there were so many mezcals there. It has completely changed in the last five years."

Today in Mexico City, spots like La Botica, Bósforo, and La Clandestina lead the charge in mezcal-focused programs. Clandestina owner Karla Moles (who also founded Mezcal Enmascarado) says that business has changed so much since 2009 that she had no trouble later opening El Palenquito and La Lavandería to meet demand. "At the beginning it was clear that the people coming in to drink mezcal were people who wanted to be different—not a bunch of sheep drinking industrial spirits," she says. "Now I can see the group of people has changed and everybody is excited about mezcal."

Kalkofen says she's seen a similar trajectory in Oaxaca. "Every time I go back there's a new mezcaleria popping up. They're opening everywhere. The younger generation is really embracing it; it's the Jack Daniel's of their generation."

Mezcaloteca's Silvia Philion says most of the interest is thanks to a cultural shift that's similar to the one that concurrently took place in America. "Eleven or

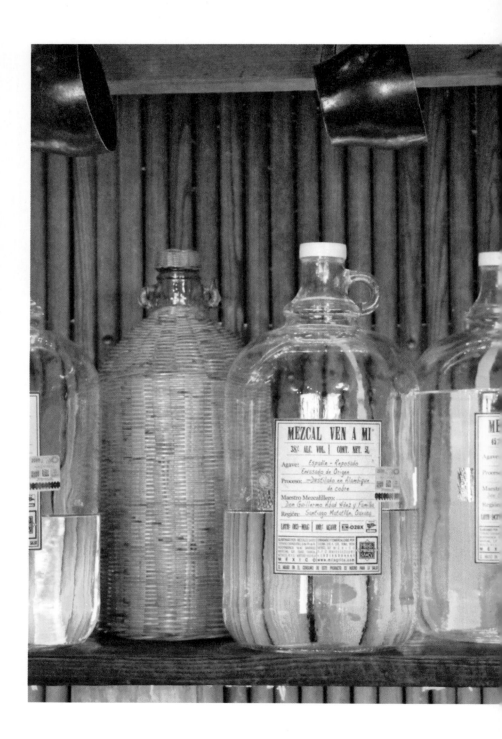

twelve years ago, the consumer started realizing he wants to buy stuff without any chemicals in the process because they're bad for your body," she says. "They want to know where everything comes from—something that's handmade from the beginning to the end, and that's mezcal. So maybe twenty years ago the consumer wouldn't appreciate mezcal. The timing now is perfect." Since Philion's bar opened, other temples of mezcal, like Ulises Torrentera's In Situ and Asis Cortés's Mezcalogia, have joined her in Oaxaca.

Interest spread to other parts of Mexico as well. When filmmaker and agave advocate Pedro Jiménez moved from Mexico City to Guadalajara in 2005, people were hardly drinking mezcal in either locale. Known more for its tequila production, Jalisco has a deep history of mezcal making, but because of the commercialization and growth of the former, mezcal production remained mostly obscure and rural. "I'd pick up mezcals from each state, wherever I went. I'd show them around at parties, and people would always say how different they are from anything they'd ever tried," Jiménez says. Inspired by the lack of options, he opened a mezcaleria called Pare de Sufrir to create a space where locals could get to know the spirit. "There's still a very small community of mezcal culture here, and now it's more like fashion and a trend than something that is cultural. But it's growing," he says.

Bottles of mezcal line the back bar at El Palenquito.

AT THE PALENQUE

In addition to traditional mezcal's booming popularity in bars, the increased demand has made a significant impact on maestro mezcaleros and their families throughout Mexico. Because drinkers on both sides of the border have taken notice, an increased number of reliable jobs for families who were otherwise struggling to make ends meet has erupted—an important economic improvement for states like Oaxaca, where 70 percent of the population lived beneath the poverty line in 2014.

The boom means different things for different producers. For some, it's simply about generating a steady source of income. At Mezcal Vago's *palenque* in Sola de Vega, it's just maestro mezcalero Salomón Rey Rodriguez in the driver's seat. Mezcal runs through "Tío" Rey's blood, but thanks to the formalization of the brand, he's one of the first on his side of the family to make mezcal full-time.

For other families where mezcal production runs deep, that kind of job security can mean keeping the family together and prospering in the face of changing economics and circumstances. This is certainly the case at Real

above: Maestro Aquilino García López's son Temo throws crushed agave fibers into a fermentation tank. He recently joined the production team at Mezcal Vago after working in Michigan and Florida for seven years.

opposite: Joel Barriga pulls some mezcal off the still to see how the flavors are developing.

above: Family photos line the wall at the Mezcal Vago palenque.

previous pages: Outside the Mezcal Vago palenque in Candelaria Yegolé, where mezcal making is a family affair.

Minero in Santa Catarina Minas—a pueblo located just outside of Oaxaca City with a subtropical microclimate—where you'll run into almost every member of the Angeles Carreño family during an afternoon at the distillery, where they've been making mezcal since the 1800s.

It's similar at Candelaria Yegolé, where Aquilino García López distills for Mezcal Vago. Here, the increase in demand has made it possible for his son, Cuautémoc (or Temo, as everyone calls him) to return home after seven years

MEZCAL IS A VERY RITUALISTIC LIQUID THAT'S INVOLVED IN A LOT OF THE TRADITIONS IN THIS PART OF THE COUNTRY. WHEN A GIRL WAS BORN INTO A FAMILY, THE FATHER PLANTED TWENTY-FIVE AGAVES AND WAITED SO HE COULD MAKE MEZCAL OUT OF THESE AGAVES TO SUPPORT HER. THAT'S THE KIND OF RELATIONSHIP PEOPLE HAVE WITH MEZCAL.

–IVÁN SALDAÑA OYARZÁBAL,
MONTELOBOS MEZCAL

of working in Michigan and Florida. When it's Aquilino's time to step aside, Temo will likely fill his shoes.

The carrying of the torch is also important to Bosscal mezcalero Uriel Simental Enriquez, a fourth-generation maestro who started learning the art of distillation at age eleven. After getting an engineering degree in agriculture in Durango City, he returned to the family distillery in Nombre de Dios to work alongside his father. "The legacy of mezcal in my family has given us so much. It provided for me as a child and now for my children," he says. "It would give me tremendous pride to see my son continue our family legacy with Bosscal and follow in my footsteps if he chooses to."

Even if mezcal doesn't run in one's lineage, many Mexican natives see the growth as a great opportunity to make a living by reconnecting with their cultural heritage. This was the case for Cecilia Murrieta of La Niña del Mezcal, and also for the cousins who started Mezcal Tosba. Elisandro and Edgar Gonzales make mezcal in a mountainous village, San Cristóbal Lachirioag, about four hours north of Oaxaca City. Elisandro works in America to make the funds necessary to feed the business as it grows, while Edgar makes the liquor back home. "I am proud of being indigenous to Mexico, and I'm not jumping into mezcal because it's a trend. It was a dream," Elisandro says. "I was raised with rum. For us to make mezcal, it's been really great." NPR picked up the Tosba story in 2014, and while the press helped the Gonzales cousins bring mezcal into a few markets, it's still a long road ahead until the business is financially viable enough for Elisandro to return home.

Francisco Javier Perez also worked in the US for several decades before getting into mezcal. In his case, the motivation emerged after returning home to help his ailing brother carry on his agave-farming business. Mezcal came next. Seeing the potential to help strengthen the community, he founded a co-op to bring agave farmers and mezcal producers together, forming Integradora Comercial de Ejutla. Now, forty-seven producers and farmers from various areas of Oaxaca are responsible for the production of Banhez mezcal. "The aim is to work with other farmers to achieve prosperity together, promote the history and tradition of mezcal, and to take care of each other," says Scott Goldman, president of CNI Brands, the company importing Banhez. Everything is made according to artisanal standards, and the resulting blend of espadín and barril is lovely. Goldman adds that more farmers are joining the co-op each month.

THE FUTURE

As demand increases on both sides of the border, it's not all sunshine and roses. A slew of concerns have emerged as new brands crowd shelves. Many of the new labels come from foreign entrepreneurs (sometimes with no stake in the culture or history of the spirit) entering the market to buy and repackage liquid under flashy names. At best, they take care of the people responsible for making this liquid gold and help preserve the cultural heritage of the spirit. At worst, they're just looking make a quick buck.

opposite: **The nursery at Wahaka Mezcal features several varieties of young agaves.**

TRANSPARENCY IS KEY

As the number of mezcal producers entering the commercial market continues to boom, labels offer one way to distinguish the traditional outfits from the mass-produced brands. If the label includes the following information, chances are the liquid inside is of reliable quality.

- Make sure the label indicates 100 percent agave.
- Labels should include the agave varietal or species.
- Quality brands will make sure a maestro mezcalero is noted.
- Where is the mezcal made? See if it lists state, village, or region.
- Each bottle must display a Norma Oficial Mexicana number (NOM)—a number linked to the exact distillery where the product is made. A quick Google search will usually bring this information to light.
- Labels on good mezcals will also include information about the types of grind, oven, fermentation vessel, and still used.
- Make sure there aren't any scorpions in the bottle.

Unlike other spirits, the distinction between these two approaches is crucial in mezcal. As demand increases, industrialization becomes a threat. As processes mechanize and speed up, people lose jobs, the flavor of the juice takes a turn towards neutral and uninspired, and the cultural knowledge of how mezcal is crafted could be lost to time forever.

Environmental concerns also abound. Remember how the agave plant can require decades to reach maturity? Unlike corn used to make whiskey, or potatoes for vodka, growth is a painfully slow process for the agaves used to make mezcal—if these plants are overharvested now to meet global demand, the industry could see shortages in the future. It's happened in the tequila industry, where cycles of abundance and shortages regularly impact the health and strength of the remaining agave crop. In mezcal, this agricultural sustainability is a tangible concern for some states, most notably where the majority of production is happening, in Oaxaca. The tobalá agave's rise in popularity a few years ago led to overharvesting the "king of agaves." Now some producers say the plant has been almost eliminated in its natural wild state.

More often than not, the responsible producers are already working towards solutions (and have been for some time). At Real Minero, Graciela Angeles Carreño started planting new agaves from seed when she was eight years old, taking care of the young plants under the supervision of her father, maestro Don Lorenzo. Since his passing in 2016, Graciela says the initiatives will remain strong to honor his legacy. "Our philosophy in planting these agaves is so the next generation can continue to propagate these plants," she says, adding the family has planted for so long they're not really worried about running out of supply. During 2016's rainy season, Real Minero planted over six thousand agaves.

Producers like Bosscal and Wahaka also plant. Like Real Minero, at the latter, maestro Alberto Morales allows the agaves to grow in the nursery for a few years, largely unbothered, and then when the plants reach a stable size and health, they are transplanted back into the wild where they can evolve at will. In 2017 Montelobos plans to branch out from the flagship espadin expression with a release made from 100 percent tobalá. "Our cultivated agave is really a semi-cultivated thing. You put the agave there and help a little bit, but you just want to take out the plants growing around, give it some space, but there's not much else you do," Saldaña Oyarzábal says.

Not every producer has their sights set on sustainability, though, and potential for a dwindling agave population merely represents one thread in a much larger tapestry of environmental issues at stake. For producers who use firewood to heat the stills, reforestation is a key topic. Pollution is another concern, as the vinasses—the liquids left over from the distillation process—are toxic if disposed of in large quantities. With a spirit category that's just starting to get its footing in a commercial world, it's a lot to consider as infrastructures are put in place.

"No one, from the smallest producer to the biggest, has the full answers of what sustainability can mean for mezcal production," says Esteban Morales Garibi, founder of La Venenosa Raicilla and Derrumbes mezcal. "There is no information or numbers about how many agaves remain in Oaxaca or other states. There is not research or money for anyone to take that to the next level. Every time I hear people talking about sustainable mezcal production, there are just more questions, no answers." A former chef, Morales Garibi works with makers in Jalisco for La Venenosa Raicilla and in many states, including San Luis Potosí, Tamaulipas, Zacatecas, and Durango, for Derrumbes, giving him a distinct perspective that those outside of Oaxaca might not bring to the table.

"A bunch of people in the industry are worried about drinking mezcal, and I say, why? These spirits exist for enjoying—to make people laugh and feel alive. Not to feel concern," he says. "There are some things to be concerned about, but it's not cool to take that and use it just for marketing"—or fear mongering, as some modern companies are apt to do.

above: Many agaves at Real Minero are allowed to sprout *quiotes*, so the crew can harvest seed pods like these.

opposite: Real Minero has a robust planting program, where they often grow agaves from seed.

These are difficult topics to discuss without either overblowing or understating the issues—especially for consumers and journalists who don't have hundreds of years of cultural knowledge under our belts. Thanks to its agricultural nature and nonindustrial production methods, the mezcal industry is fragile, and right now it's at a crossroads, so it's important for producers to talk about these issues and find a path forward. On the other hand, as Morales Garibi hints, these issues are just that: considerations to be figured out, not reasons for consumers to quit drinking mezcal to protect its future. "If we're going to spend the time talking about the issues and not the people who really know how to do this, these people will stop doing it. If we lose the people, we lose the knowledge and then we lose mezcal," Garibi says. "We could have a happy forest full of agaves without any mezcalero." Wouldn't that be ironic?

As long as producers remain mindful of their environmental footprints, we're looking at a bright future. In a decade (or maybe less), hundreds of different mezcal expressions hailing from different states will enter the Mexican and American markets (we'll likely see other Mexican spirits, like *sotol*, take flight, too). If we as consumers keep our heads on straight and vote with our pocketbooks, we can help ensure this scenario occurs without strife.

"Each one of us, as consumers, can contribute to conserving the natural and cultural wealth of mezcals by choosing to consume the products of small, local producers who use environmentally responsible and culturally conscious methods," says biologist Catarina Illsley Granich in an *Artes de México* essay called "Keys to Savoring Mezcals." "Together, we can advance toward a new tradition of mezcals that recognizes and values the great diversity characterizing us as a country."

PART TWO

THE NUTS

& BOLTS

Rooted to the earth like living monoliths, amid a landscape that seems to conspire against hope, the magueys watch as generations of men come and go, one after the other. Their spiky leaves rimmed with thorns and their succulent hearts hold all the wisdom of a world without urgency, without tricks or traps. And because of that, when the maguey sap is running through our veins, we are overcome by a sense of wisdom and eternity.

—Fausto Rasero, *Artes de México #98*:
Mezcal Arte Tradicional

Spiky agaves of all shapes and sizes stick out from Yagul's overgrown ruins like pincushions marking the winding paths. It's a balmy October afternoon, and I'm with a group of liquor distributors on a plateau at one of the higher points of the UNESCO-recognized archeological site in central Oaxaca. Together, we're overlooking the surrounding Sierras and listening to the booming voice of Iván Saldaña Oyarzábal carry over the warm breeze. He's explaining how the natural conditions of the valley have shaped the biological makeup of agave and, by proxy, the flavor of mezcal.

The passionate, bespectacled character commanding our attention is one of the world's foremost specialists in agave. Saldaña Oyarzábal's 2013 book *Anatomy of Mezcal*, still serves as one of the best resources for detailing how

opposite: One of several ways agave plants reproduce is via seed. A quiote, or tall stalk, shoots up from the center of the plant with seed pods growing out of the top.

the agave plant affects the taste and processes of making mezcal. Hailing from Guadalajara and holding a PhD in biochemistry from the University of Sussex in England, he is also a producer. As the cofounder of Montelobos (and sister spirit Ancho Reyes), he's responsible for helping transform the plant from raw material into liquid with the help of partner Don Abel Lopez.

Saldaña Oyarzábal explains that in order to fully understand mezcal, as with most distilled spirits, the conversation must start with the raw material. Trace the word *agave* back to its linguistic roots, and the path will lead you to the Greek word *agauos,* meaning "noble." And a regal plant it is. The agave's role as the core of rural communities reaches as far back as the region's recorded history, with records indicating its use for medicine, food, building materials, textiles, and more.

Still used for these purposes in some rural areas of Mexico, the plant is now better known as the source of many tasty liquids, like the sugary sweet *aguamiel*, tangy fermented *pulque*, and of course, mezcal. Ask Saldaña Oyarzábal *why* the maguey makes the world's most complex spirit, and you'll get an earful. "Agaves have been in this continent from the very beginning, eleven or twelve million years ago. Humans just arrived twelve thousand years ago, so agaves have grown and appeared independently from human beings," he says. "This is very different from grapes or wheat or barley or rye. Agaves were here by themselves developing."

Yagul is a UNESCO-recognized archeological site in central Oaxaca.

The agave is a succulent that struggles to live and lives to struggle—this rugged individualism is one of the main reasons why mezcal tastes so special, he says. If you know anything about wine, you might have heard a similar mantra: grapes that grow under difficult conditions make better vintages. The same goes for the agave. "Without pain, agave cannot achieve greatness," Saldaña Oyarzábal says. "It is through suffering that the plant produces the ideal botanical elements that give us taste."

Another reason why the agave plant makes for such interesting liquid is its sheer diversity of varieties. Of the 150 to 250 species thriving throughout North America, Mexico, South America, and parts of the Caribbean, the vast majority grow in Mexico, and up to 50 are used to make mezcal (though that figure still fluctuates, depending on the biologist cited). Tequila can be made from just a single variety of agave: blue weber, which limits its span of flavors. Imagine the number of potential outcomes for mezcal flavors based on the number of plant varieties alone.

The notion of terroir also comes into play with mezcal. A term used frequently in the wine sphere, terroir refers to the way environmental factors impart characteristics and flavors to the final beverage. Everything from soil, water, elevation, climate, and other ecosystems can make a difference. With agave, a scientific link between raw material and the expression of terroir hasn't been formally connected yet, but many scientists and producers subscribe to the idea anyway. Because of the plant's extremely long lifespan, it's impossible to imagine the fibers would not soak up the essence of where the maguey is grown.

Imagine if a pinot noir grape took thirty-five years to mature, like the mighty *tepeztate* agave does. The sense of place in the final bottle would be insane. "Agaves are definitely one of the plants that exhibit terroir. It's one of the most extraordinary things," Saldaña Oyarzábal says, adding that few other distilled spirits exhibit the same ground-to-bottle characteristics. "It's like a long photographic exposure of their conditions, because they have such a long lifespan."

Time. Suffering. Terroir. Consider how these aspects lumped together might influence a finished batch of mezcal. An espadín from Oaxaca could

above: Oftentimes distilleries are bare-bones operations located in remote areas. Many, like this palenque in Santa Catarina Minas, make mezcal only for the surrounding village and not under a formal label or brand.

below: Montelobos founder Iván Saldaña Oyarzábal is an authority on the history of the agave and how its characteristics influence mezcal flavors.

taste totally different than one from Puebla, which could taste different than one made in Guerrero. At a single distillery, mezcal made from tobalá will taste totally different than one made with *arroqueño*. If a tepeztate is harvested for mezcal production at twenty years, it could perhaps taste younger or less interesting than one harvested at thirty. The sky's the limit when it comes to flavor variations, and for mezcal nerds like Saldaña Oyarzábal (and me), that's just layers and layers of appeal setting the stage for a great-tasting mezcal.

Montelobos mezcal is made with the espadín variety of agave, pictured here. Espadín agaves come from the *angustifolia* species. In mezcal, they often yield a fine balance between sweetness and herbaceousness.

THE SPECIES

The following rundown describes some of the more common agave species used to make mezcal today. The list is by no means comprehensive, but rather a snapshot of trends in the current market. Most agave scientists and biologists argue against making generalizations about what each agave species contributes to mezcal in terms of final flavor. As previously described, every plant—even those within the same species—can yield different results depending on where it was grown and how it was processed.

That said, it doesn't hurt to take a stab at what flavors certain agaves might yield in a finished mezcal to help you navigate the complicated waters of mezcal. The flavor notes below were compiled from a variety of observations made by bartenders, brand owners, and yours truly. Take 'em with a grain of salt.

AGAVE ANGUSTIFOLIA

Perhaps the most widely distributed species of mezcal-friendly agave, *angustifolia* is the parent of the espadín variety—to date, the most common mezcal exported to the United States. Striking a refined balance between sweetness and herbaceousness, the medium-sized espadín typically takes somewhere from five to nine years to mature. It is easily cultivated throughout Oaxaca, Michoacán, Durango, and Puebla, where it's called *espadilla*. In Sonora, mezcal made from the *angustifolia* species is designated as bacanora, since the state doesn't land within the formal Appellation of Origin for mezcal. Newcomers should start with an espadín for its exceptional balance and friendly personality.

BOTTLES TO TRY:

Del Maguey Santo Domingo Albarradas

Choosing a favorite expression from Del Maguey is a tough call, but the fresh tropical pineapple, underlying smoke, and dark chocolate bark notes of the Albarradas from maestro Espiridion Morales Luis gets me every time.

Alipus Santa Ana Del Rio

Sweet like a juicy pear or a crunchy slice of jicama, this espadín has a booming structure with pecks of black pepper and a clean, saline-filled finish. Spirits connoisseur Paul Pacult gave the release four stars, and I'm inclined to agree.

Mezcal Koch Espadín Olla de Barro

Distilled in clay pots (*olla de barro*), this aggressive espadín tastes like jagged slate and river rock, with hints of green herbs and coconut peering up from the depths. The producers at Koch pay special attention to issues like water use, agave availability, and forestry resources, so they're a solid group to support.

AGAVE AMERICANA VAR. OAXACENSIS

The enormous arroqueño is probably the most common variety of the *Agave americana* species used to make mezcal. Grown wild and cultivated, the towering plant with spiky arms closely resembles the smaller espadín at first glance, but grows much larger in scale and takes up to twenty years to reach maturity. *Oaxacensis* subvarieties used to make mezcal that can be found bottled and exported include **coyote** and **sierra negra**.

BOTTLES TO TRY:

Siete Misterios Coyote

I first tried Siete Misterios on my honeymoon in Mexico City, and I fell in love with everything about the brand, from its appealing label design to the liquid inside. Round and earthy from distillation in clay pots, this coyote is a special one. Chocolate, warm squash, and dusty ash lead the flavor, which ends on the sweet side instead of acidic.

Del Maguey Arroqueño

Reminiscent of what I imagine a very old, wise espadín might taste like, the arroqueño from Del Maguey has elements of damp forest floor with a pinch of cardamom for interest. Made with agaves left to mature for eight to twelve years, the mezcal feels a touch young, but not in a bad way—it's complex and vegetal with a long finish.

AGAVE CUPREATA

Endemic to the Balsas River basin in Guerrero, but also grown at high elevations in Michoacán, Guerrero, and Puebla (with smaller pockets of production sprouting up in Oaxaca), *cupreata* is a shorter, squat plant that's also called *papalometl*, *papalote*, *chino*, *ancho*, and *papalome*, depending on where it's grown. Usually wild (states like Guerrero are quickly starting to cultivate), *cupreata* makes light-bodied mezcal that tends to have a bright, floral character, sometimes with a piney, resinous finish.

BOTTLES TO TRY:

Mezcales de Leyenda Guerrero

You might recognize Leyenda by its signature squatty bottle. The goods inside are even more appealing. In the fresh *cupreata* expression from Guerrero, clean pineapple, tropical fruits, and bananas lead the charge.

Mayalen Guerrero

On the more burly side with 54 percent alcohol by volume. But don't let the proof scare you away from this earthy mezcal. It's savory and salty like fish and chips with malt vinegar, and the appealing layers of complexity are fun to unpack with each sip.

AGAVE MARMORATA

Old and wise, the tepeztate, or **tepextate**, variety of *Agave marmorata* can take up to thirty-five years to reach maturity. It's not uncommon to find one of the enormous plants, with its wild, lumbering arms, crawling out of the side of a mountain or rock face like an ominous green spider. Because they take so long to mature, the terroir is explicit, with fresh jalapeño and bell pepper notes dominating the aromas, and an extremely herbaceous personality emerging on the palate. *Marmorata* agaves are typically found in the more arid areas of Oaxaca, Puebla, Michoacán, and other parts of central and southern Mexico. Most commonly found wild, it makes for truly special mezcal.

BOTTLES TO TRY:

Del Maguey Wild Tepextate

Wild plants form the foundation of this gorgeous mezcal, made by the same producer of Del Maguey's famed tobalá (who remains anonymous). Layers of flavor unfold like an artichoke, with marzipan and bright basil battling for attention on a base of sweet canela, or Mexican cinnamon. A special-occasion bottle if there ever was one.

Marca Negra Tepeztate

Distilled in copper pots in Oaxaca, the *marmorata* expression from Marca Negra is made in San Luis Del Rio by maestro Jorge Mendez. A terrific balance of savory and sweet.

opposite: The mighty arroqueño plant can take up to twenty years to reach maturity.

AGAVE KARWINSKII

With thick, woody stalks and a spiky cluster of *pencas* (leaves) punctuating the top (like a flaming matchstick instead of a rotund succulent), *Agave karwinskii* is an oddball that looks kind of like a Muppet. Several varieties in the *karwinskii* species are used to make mezcal, including *madre-cuishe, barril, cirial,* and *largo*, and because the fibrous stalks are often incorporated in the cooking and fermentation processes, the mezcals taste stone dry with plenty of wine-like tannins.

BOTTLES TO TRY:

Rey Campero Madre-Cuishe

One of my all-time favorites, this chocolatey madre-cuishe is a 48.6 percent ABV treasure from maestro Romulo Sanchez Parada in Candelaria Yegolé, Oaxaca. All of the classic goodness of *karwinskii* comes out in this release, with a dry, thyme-like herbal quality supported by plentiful threads of smoke.

Real Minero Largo

On the tangier end of the spectrum, Real Minero's clay-pot-distilled Largo mezcal sings with high lemon-peel notes, rooted in a smack of roasted agave fibers that taste kind of like sweet potato and charcoal.

El Jolgorio Tobaziche

The spirits reviewer from Astor Wines (www.astorwines.com) calls Jolgorio's maestro "one of the living gods of the mezcal world," and this explosive release is a great example of why. The 100 percent wild tobaziche expression made in Lachigui almost transcends time and place, with a wellspring of flavors that oscillates between pine needles, underripe banana, and zesty lemon with a big blast of smoke and young pumpkin on the finish.

AGAVE RHODACANTHA

More delicate in body and flavor, the *rhodacantha* species can bring a lovely floral, honey-like quality to mezcal, oftentimes ending in a fleeting finish. The *mexicano* variety grows from Sonora south to Oaxaca, mostly in the foothills of the highlands, and is also called *dobadan* or *dobadaan* in various Zapotec dialects. Some take ten to twelve years to mature.

opposite: A fruitful species, the *karwinskii* species looks totally different than most mezcal agaves, with a long woody stalk and spiky arms sprouting from the top.

BOTTLES TO TRY:

El Jolgorio Mexicano

Feathery light in texture, with a pronounced raisin-like quality, this mezcal was made by maestro Ignacio Parada using eight-year-old *mexicano* plants. An ideal place to start for those looking for something subtle, with a substantial smoke element still present.

Marca Negra Dobadán

Wild agaves were smashed with wooden mallets and distilled twice in a copper still to make this pretty mezcal. It's a subtle, well-balanced expression with strong cooked agave flavors, and grapefruit peel and brown sugar rounding out the complexity.

Mezcalero Special Bottling No. 2

Made exclusively from wild Dobadaan, this piquant mezcal was distilled in 2012 and set aside for three years prior to bottling and distribution. Cinnamon and kiwi emerge first on the palate, finishing in an alpine-like burst of green. Mezcalero expressions tend to be special releases thanks to the use of the wild agave (which is also harder to find and slightly more expensive than others), but across the board, they show a restrained elegance, with big agave flavors. Good to hunt down regardless of the current varietal release.

AGAVE POTATORUM

The petite agave best known as tobalá was one of the first wild varietals to hit America after espadín entered, when Del Maguey's Ron Cooper brought his special version into the country. "Only God plants tobalá," Cooper says. "It grows in the shade of trees like truffles. It takes fifteen years to mature." In other words, a truly special agave. Since the height of their popularity, these short, geometric plants have largely been overharvested in Oaxaca. Some producers cultivate to help resurrect the shortage, and crops remain viable in certain areas of Puebla. If you do snag a bottle, expect a high price tag because of the availability, size, and stunning flavor—tobalá makes for mezcal with a woody, sometimes fruity personality and a sweet, enduring finish.

opposite: Madre-cuishe agaves at the Wahaka Mezcal nursery.

Tobalá are one of the most popular agaves used to make mezcal. Some call them the "kings of mezcal."

BOTTLES TO TRY:

Tosba Tobalá

Highly floral with a slightly salty character, this tobalá was made in Lachirioag—a mountainous area about four hours north of Oaxaca City—by maestro Edgar Gonzalez. Tosba prevents overharvesting of the plant and is working on building nurseries to cultivate for future generations, so don't feel guilty when you get your hands on a bottle.

La Niña del Mezcal Tobalá

Another mezcal brand with a great backstory, La Niña's tobalá captures the essence of the agave's spirit, with sweet honeysuckle, fresh grass, and warm vanilla making up the tapestry of flavors.

AGAVE TEQUILANA

The species known primarily for its use in tequila production, *tequilana* is at times processed in a way that's more aligned with traditional mezcal. This creates a spirit that tastes how tequila probably did before the commercialization of the industry. Outside of Jalisco, the variety grows well in Michoacán and Zacatecas.

BOTTLES TO TRY:

Del Maguey San Luis del Rio Azul
Dense with personality, yet crisp and refreshing. You'd never guess this was the same plant responsible for tequila production. Azul tastes like wet stones, lemon peel, and white peppercorn.

Fidencio Mezcal Único
The first release from Fidencio has been in and out of production. The higher proof allows the personality of the *tequilana* to shine through, proving this varietal has so much more to say than most tequila producers allow.

Siembra Valles Ancestral
A groundbreaking release from the Siembra Valles team, Ancestral is made in Jalisco, but processed in earthen pit ovens and distilled in pine and copper. Since the plants are from an area flush with volcanic soil, the mineral character is pronounced, with bright citrus high notes and a peppery finish.

AGAVE INAEQUIDENS

Grown largely in pine forests and on mountain slopes, *inaequidens* is one of the main species used to make raicilla in Jalisco and mezcal in Michoacán. It's also known for the production of mead and pulque in the center of the country.

BOTTLES TO TRY:

La Venenosa Sierra del Tigre de Jalisco Raicilla
The raicilla releases from La Venenosa are horses of different colors. Each boasts an explosive amount of flavor that's at times hard to characterize outside of the impression of being "funky." In this one, I pick up flavors like cherry, rosemary, smoky sour cream, and fresh goat cheese. Mmm.

Don Mateo de la Sierra Alto
Made in Michoacán, this mezcal gains added complexity after distillation in a hybrid still made of pine and copper. It's an elegant blend of tropical kiwi, white pepper, lavender, and mesquite.

AGAVE SALMIANA
Popular in the states of San Luis Potosí, Zacatecas, Guanajuato, and Tamaulipas, the *salmiana* agave produces a very low yield, meaning it can require up to four times as much plant as *tequilana* to create the same amount of product.

BOTTLE TO TRY:
Derrumbes San Luis Potosí
One of the only mezcal bottles in the US that hails from San Luis Potosí, wild *salmiana* lends flavors of celery, olives, and chili peppers. Cooked in aboveground ovens, it has a distinct lack of smoke; instead, a somewhat chalky finish hints at the terroir of the high altitudes where the plant was harvested.

AGAVE CONVALLIS
A spiky plant with thorns that resemble the tusks of the wild boar, *jabalí* agaves are notoriously finicky to work with, as the plant thrives in difficult cliffs and rocks (average maturity level takes ten to twelve years) and can cause a foamy ruckus during fermentation and distillation. Yet instead of tasting rugged and unrefined, jabalí makes for gorgeous mezcal.

BOTTLES TO TRY:
Wahaka Mezcal Jabalí
I used to think Wahaka's *ensamble* was my favorite label from the brand. And then I met jabalí. Minty and herbaceous, it's got enough punch to remind you of the burly raw material, but finishes in such a soft kiss of spice and fruit that it's smart to revisit each sip from start to finish so the experience doesn't have to end.

opposite: *Jabalí* is an agave from the *convallis* species. It's difficult to work with but makes for extremely expressive mezcal.

Rey Campero Jabalí

A big burst of salty watermelon leads the charge in this beaming mezcal from Rey Campero. Cantaloupe, walnut, and almonds round out the flavor profile, and a downright succulent, damp quality twists and turns through moments of dank smoke.

AGAVE DURANGENSIS

Native to Durango and also found in parts of Zacatecas, wild *durangensis* agaves, like the *cenizo* variety, grow abundantly in the arid scrublands and forests. It's mostly wild, but semicultivation is starting in the area for sustainability purposes. The plants vary greatly in size and in the shape of the broad leaves, so things like sugar content can range wildly between those grown in desert-like climates and those grown in the warmer, wetter areas.

BOTTLES TO TRY:

Bosscal Mezcal

Made in the heart of Nombre de Dios (which means "name of God" in English), the cenizo release from Bosscal Mezcal is unique because the agaves are fermented in underground vats and distilled in wooden tanks.

Mezcales de Leyenda Durango

A shock of crisp, clean lemon and slate flavors melt into sweet peach and rosemary in this herbaceous release, also from Nombre de Dios. Mezcales de Leyenda are certified organic by the USDA and CCOF in Mexico.

ENSAMBLES

While single-variety mezcals are most popular right now, the past (and quite possibly the future) of mezcal largely consisted of blends. *Ensambles* were the logical choice because the mezcaleros would simply go foraging for whatever was ripe and available. Though single varieties have since come into favor, the sheer complexity of blends makes an easy argument for their consumption.

BOTTLES TO TRY:

Banhez

One of the most flavorful entry-level mezcals out there hails from San Miguel Ejutla. The mezcal isn't made by a single mezcalero but rather a co-op composed mostly of agave farmers. A blend of 90 percent seven-year-old

Mezcal tobalá has been overharvested in many areas of Oaxaca, so producers are starting to plant semicultivated crops to revive the variety.

espadín and twelve-year-old barril provides an interplay of sweet and dry, with a round body. A friendly handshake to the category of ensambles.

Real Minero Ensamble Blanco Tobalá, Largo, and Barril

If you make it down to Mexico, seek out this jewel. Yes, a whopping four different varieties of agave define this *en barro* release from the Santa Catarina Minas distillery. Honeycomb leads the aroma, which sidesteps into a thick layer of Scotch-like smoke, dry walnuts, and roasted tomato. The entanglement of layers is unmatched.

THE ALCHEMY

Mezcalero Salomón Rey Rodriguez sometimes sleeps in a hammock in his palenque so that in the middle of the night he can stoke the fires that heat the stills.

As we walk into the sparse, open-air room where he produces Mezcal Vago's tobalá and most of the ensambles, Rodriguez pulls up a few chairs and flashes a weary-but-welcoming smile. The fifty-seven-year-old mezcalero is tired after hosting a dozen touring bartenders the day before, preparing for Día de los Muertos rituals and tending to the mezcal every few hours overnight. Nevertheless, he offers us a welcome mezcal and *cervecita*—a petite bottle of Corona—and starts joking around with Francisco Terrazas, brand and operations manager and our tour guide for the day. Hospitality in Oaxaca knows no bounds.

Hammocks are a common sight at distilleries around Mexico, because mezcal-making at the artisanal and ancestral level can be a tiresome, laborious, around-the-clock operation. In small rural outfits like Vago's, production is also far from modern. There aren't thermometers and knobs and dials and conveyor belts and mechanical shredders like one might find in a Kentucky bourbon distillery—just wooden fermentation vats, seasoned stills, and sometimes plastic bins for storing hooch. The mezcalero—not a machine—oversees every moment of production, and in the case of Tío Rey, sometimes it's only the mezcalero running the ship. Every decision he makes is informed by tradition, and most are made out of necessity instead of innovation.

Each of the million tiny decisions that happen from plant to bottle has the potential to impact the blueprint of a batch, meaning every mezcal will have a unique personality. It's what those in the business call "the hand of the maker." Consistency isn't always the name of the game at these kinds of distilleries (though that shifts when you talk about industrial production), as it might be with whiskey or gin. It's the personality of the mezcalero, his family traditions, and practical decisions that make a difference. It's one more part of the puzzle that makes this spirit so varied and exciting.

"An espadín from Tío Rey in Sola de Vega, where he crushes by hand and distills in clay pots—that's going to taste drastically different than the espadín from Aquilino in Candelaria Yegolé," says Terrazas. "Tío Rey's [mezcals] tend to be savory and spicy, where Aquilino's tend to be more elegant and refined. When I'm tasting with people, whether it's at a bar or what, I try to explain that it's very much a case of the maker's personality coming out."

As we dig into the different ways mezcaleros make their magic happen, it's important to keep in mind that there's no right way or wrong way to make mezcal. Some stick to traditions passed on through the generations. Others look for ways to adapt and evolve as the demands of the industry increase. Some manage to achieve a balance. Others experiment and innovate for the fun of it. In this section, I'll focus mostly on ancestral and artisanal methods (see sidebar on page 81), because quite frankly, industrial mass-production is boring and the resulting products lack charisma.

Also, as we go through each step of the process, note the flavor graphs included in each section. One of the most sophisticated things you can do when drinking mezcal is learn to think beyond the smoke. Not only is there a wide spectrum of intensity across brands, but also many other personalities can be discovered in mezcal as a result of the intricacies of the process. Iván Saldaña Oyarzábal investigates this idea as part of his excellent treatise on mezcal, *The Anatomy of Mezcal,* wherein he matches final flavors to the step of production where they originate. Inspired by his legwork—and with a little help from barkeeps around the US—in each section, I've included some characteristics to look for when sipping.

GROWING AND HARVESTING

The first step in making mezcal is sourcing and harvesting the plants. Historically, most producers would seek out ripe and ready agaves from their own lands. Everything grew wild, and the resulting mezcal would be made from a number of varieties cooked and blended together to make an *ensamble*.

Now, single-varietal expressions are the style du jour. This type of production requires more planning and sometimes a deliberate cultivation of plants in order to make sure there will be enough of a certain type ready for cooking at the same time. Some producers simply buy raw agave plants from farmers or brokers to reach quantities needed to cook a batch. Others finagle a blend of the two methods—using wild and cultivated agaves from their own lands and buying a mixture of both from brokers.

Regardless of where the plants come from, the key to good mezcal is to use only agaves that have reached full maturity. Once the plants are ready, *palenqueros* (distillery workers), hack the sharp leaves away from the plant, leaving just the heart, or *piña*, behind for cooking. These rotund, pineapple-looking hearts, which range from ten to hundreds of pounds each depending on the species or variety, are then hacked into quarters or halves to prepare for cooking.

How much *penca*, or leaf, is shaved off is a decision left up to the maestro and his palenqueros. Sometimes a fair amount is included with the plant, which can contribute a pronounced bitter quality. Other times, it's trimmed

above: Tío Rey's hammock at Mezcal Vago. He often awakes at night to keep the roasting fires stoked.

opposite: At Montelobos, a *palenquero* chops large agave hearts into more manageable sizes. Every agave is chopped into either halves or quarters to prepare for cooking.

below: Raw *karwinskii* agaves harvested and ready to roast.

as close to the white piña as possible for sweetness. In the case of *Agave karwinskii*, because of its unusual spear-like shape, the woody stalks are often incorporated into a roast, contributing a whole new complexity.

THE ROAST

Once harvested, agave plants must be cooked to soften the fibers and transform starches into sugars that can be easily fermented. Like a delicious butternut squash that's been cooking in an oven for hours, this is the part of the process that creates mezcal's darkest savory elements. It's also why some mezcal tastes strongly of smoke.

In many traditional and artisanal outfits, cooking is done in either a stone or clay masonry oven (common in San Luis Potosí, Jalisco, and Zacatecas), or in a deep, conical pit carved out of the earth (often seen in Oaxaca and Guerrero). The hole is lined with stone and wood, which is lit and left to burn until the maestro determines the correct temperature has been achieved. *Bagasse*, the agave fibers left over from previous distillations, are spread over the fire so the piñas don't burn directly on the wood or coals. At this point, each raw, heavy piña is strategically organized in the pit. The largest chunks stay closest to the fire, and the smallest piñas rest near the top, so everything cooks evenly. Palenqueros then cover the pile with a tarp or dirt, and sometimes a cross to ward away evil spirits (see sidebar, page 92). In underground or earthen ovens, the piñas are left to cook for three to five days.

Some companies make expressions that are steamed instead of roasted as a way to explore the pure flavors of mezcal without the interference of smoke. Though it caught some flak when it first launched, Fidencio's Único is a good example of this. "People called it an American mezcal, which wasn't true, because [producer] Esteban was already making it before I started working with him,"

THREE CATEGORIES OF CLASSIFICATION

In early 2017, the Mexican government updated the guidelines that define mezcal production, addressing an argument that's been going on for years in the ether of the Internet. With the update, three formal tiers of classification were passed into law: ancestral, artisanal, and industrial. The distinction is important because the lines blur as modern producers and brand owners start to take liberties with tradition and introduce new technologies. Now they can run but they can't hide. Here's how it works.

ANCESTRAL The most rustic and rudimentary version of mezcal production. Agaves must be cooked in earthen pit ovens; milled by a *tahona* (a stone wheel), an Egyptian mill, or mallets; and fermented in one of a variety of vessel options, including wood, clay, animal skins, or tree trunks. Fermentation must include the fibers from the crushed maguey. Distillation must be in clay pots over direct fire and must also include agave fibers.

ARTISANAL Artisanal production is a clean and natural process, similar to ancestral. However, in artisanal production, agaves can be cooked in stone ovens in addition to earthen pits and can be milled by mechanical shredders too. Shredders are a key gripe for opponents because modern technology rarely yields the most flavorful results. For fermentation, the vessels must be the same as ancestral, but the key factor is that the maguey fibers can, but don't have to, be used. Distillation can be in clay or copper stills, and may (not must) include the maguey fibers.

INDUSTRIAL These large-scale productions typically make mezcal for the masses, sometimes using diffusers and autoclaves to cook the plants. They produce largely flavorless stuff that's typically too smoky and can be cut with sugar and water to extend batches. By law, production at this level allows for grinding with shredders or series of mills, fermentation in stainless-steel tanks, and the use of column or continuous stills made with either copper or stainless steel. How to avoid this mass-produced, tasteless junk? Check labels for detailed information on who makes the spirit, where it's made, what kinds of tools are used, and other details. Good brands will be transparent about these issues, which usually correlates to honest and delicious mezcal.

above: Don Bernardo Morales, father of maestro Alberto Morales, at Wahaka Mezcal, shows off a roasted agave fresh from the pit.

previous pages: This mound of raw agaves is almost ready to be covered with dirt and finished.

founder and partner Arik Torren explains. "I got excited about the fact that he was innovative as well as traditional, because everything else about it is traditional."

On an industrial scale, steaming is a negative when autoclaves and diffusers are used to expedite the process. These large machines combine many steps into one, using high-pressure water, shredders, and sometimes sulfuric acid to extract sugar for fermentation. The results for both processes are bland, oftentimes dimensionless mezcal. Luckily, diffusers are typically seen only at the very large industrial level.

Regardless of process, the smoke element shouldn't be too overpowering once you get to know the spirit. In fact, too much smoke can be a defect in

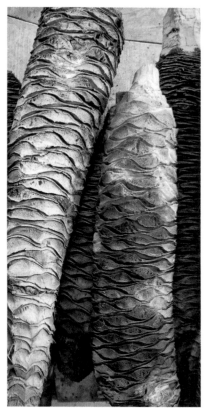

left: Roasted agave looks very different after it's removed from the ovens. If you taste the fibers at this point, flavors of toffee, squash, and caramel are common.

right: Cooked *karwinskii* agaves rest before being crushed.

production or worse: an intentional over-roasting intended to appeal to a market where smoke is the only thing they talk about in relation to mezcal. Let's help reverse the potential for that outcome by looking for the other flavors that can emerge as a result of the roasting. You'll sound way cooler than your friends if your vocabulary goes beyond "It's so smoky."

THE GRIND

After the piñas spend time cooling after the roast, the maestro checks each chunk to make sure it hasn't been overcooked or developed any unpleasant molds while sitting in the sun. Then the massive hearts are pulverized to

FLAVOR NOTES FROM THE ROAST

Visit any mezcal distillery and your tour guide will likely offer you a taste of freshly roasted agave. Fibrous and warm, flavors of honey, toffee, pumpkin, and acorn squash come through the stringy fibers. Thanks to the caramelization of sugars, the cooking process also yields notes that may include sweet potato, smoke, squash, caramel, walnut, peanut, almond, hazelnut, and brown sugar. Other flavors that can emerge from roasting are bittersweet coffee beans, dried chili peppers, ash, charcoal, pepper, tannins, chocolate, wood, and fire.

extract the sticky sugars and juices. In parts of Guerrero, Michoacán, Puebla, and some remote areas of Oaxaca, this is commonly done by hand with an axe or a weighty baseball bat–looking mallet. Mezcaleros and their kin spend hours upon hours (sometimes eight to twelve per batch) smashing cooked agave hearts into strips of fiber thin enough to go into the fermentation tanks. In other areas of Oaxaca and southern Puebla, the work is outsourced to donkeys and mules. At the Montelobos palenque in Santiago Matatlán, a weathered, somewhat grumpy creature named Rambo pulls a multiton stone wheel called a *tahona*

right: Wheelbarrows of cooked agave go from the pit to the crushing floor.

PEOPLE HAVE THIS BADGE OF HONOR BASED ON HOW MANY WRINKLES AND HOW BAD YOUR PRODUCER LOOKS–THIS ROMANTIC IDEA OF A GUY WHO MAKES THREE LITERS A YEAR AND HAD TO SACRIFICE HIS SECOND BORN–BUT IT'S NOT LIKE THAT. THIS GUY IS WORKING HARD. HE'S MAKING A LIVING BY MAKING BEAUTIFUL MEZCALES. YOU HAVE TO ADAPT.

–DANNY MENA, MEZCALES DE LEYENDA

in a shallow circular pit to make the mash. Around and around, the stubborn animal turns until the fibers are crushed into a gooey pulp.

Milling can also be carried out by mechanical shredders. This technology is used for efficiency in larger, modern distilleries. As with most contemporary techniques, it's a point of dispute with traditionalists, but Mezcales de Leyenda partner Danny Mena puts the topic into perspective when he says the only person who might be able to tell the difference in flavor between hand-milled and machine-milled is the maestro. "The agaves in Guerrero used to be all hand-crushed, and now most—including ours—are using a mechanical till. The flavors are the same," he says.

FERMENTATION

After the piñas are properly ground, it's time for the sugars to be converted into alcohol by way of fermentation. This is one of the most exciting (and admittedly nerdy) parts of mezcal production because so many variables come into play. More often than not, the fibers and juices are shoveled into fermentation vessels, water is added, and the batch is left alone for the wild yeasts to do their thing. In artisanal and ancestral production, the yeasts are indigenous and wild. That's the basic version.

previous pages: Mules often drag a weighty concrete stone, or tahona, over roasted agaves to crush them into a juicy mash for fermentation. Here, Montelobos's mule, Rambo, pulls the tahona.

opposite: The fermentation process sometimes takes place in large wooden vats, like this one.

BY THE GRACE OF GOD

Little jewels of spirituality and ritual can be found throughout mezcal production. At places like Montelobos, maestro Don Abel Lopez fills his hat with dried chili peppers for good luck and spreads them over the fire before the pit is sealed. If you've toasted chili peppers at home, recall the stinging smoky aromas this creates—perfect for warding off evil spirits and curses, right? At Real Minero, a prayer is said over the cook, and crosses are planted near every step of the facility, from the top of the dirt-covered pit to the fermentation tanks.

MEZCALES TRADICIONALES
LOS PUEBLOS DE MÉXICO

above: For some, spirituality comes into play at various stages of production. Here, at the Real Minero distillery, former maestro Don Lorenzo insisted that crosses be staged near the fermentation tanks.

right: A Nahuatl saying on the wall of the Real Minero palenque touts the rewards that will come to those who are good stewards of the earth.

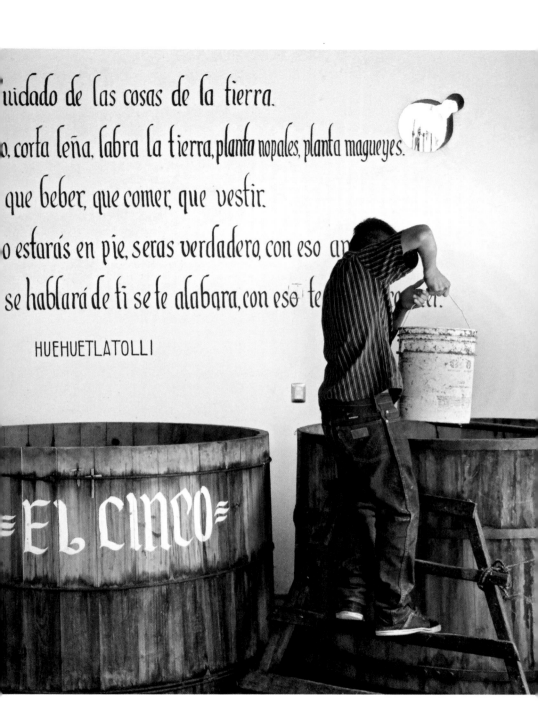

uidado de las cosas de la tierra.

o, corta leña, labra la tierra, planta nopales, planta magueyes.

que beber, que comer, que vestir.

o estarás en pie, seras verdadero, con eso a

se hablará de ti se te alabara, con eso te

HUEHUETLATOLLI

EL CINCO

The type of vessel used plays a big role in what kinds of yeasts and bacteria get to work and how drastically temperature fluctuates within, which in turn changes the flavors and aromas of the liquid. Fermentation vessels come in all shapes, sizes, and materials. In Oaxaca, large wooden vats are typical. In some areas, like parts of Jalisco, Durango, and Nayarit, fermentation takes place in underground pits for better temperature control (and thus a consistent final product). Ceramic is a traditional, ancestral vessel that's still used just north of Oaxaca City; elsewhere, stainless steel is on the rise. Some producers use plastic, an inexpensive but uninspired option. But the vessel that really gets mezcal lovers in a tizzy is rawhide. "The leather has a big influence on the flavor," says Erick Rodríguez of Almamezcalera. The rogue entrepreneur spends most of his time traveling throughout Mexico, seeking out indigenous productions and bringing very special, limited releases to the States. He's seen fermentation in rawhide in parts of Puebla, Oaxaca, and Sonora. "The aromas and flavors get a lot more busy, with stronger yeast qualities and a lot more complexity. Sometimes there's a buttery aftertaste," he says.

> # IN MEZCAL, NOTHING IS QUICK. IT REQUIRES A LOT OF PATIENCE. EVEN WITH COOKING AND FERMENTATIONS, YOU CAN'T RUSH THINGS. YOU HAVE TO LET EVERYTHING TAKE THE TIME THAT IT NEEDS.
>
> **–GRACIELA ANGELES CARREÑO, REAL MINERO**

FLAVOR NOTES FROM FERMENTATION

An untamed collection of wild yeast and bacteria that sparks the process of converting sugars into alcohol adds countless layers of interesting flavors. When you find fruity notes like banana, pineapple, ripe red berries, dried fruit, and mango—or nail polish or leather—it's likely from fermentation.

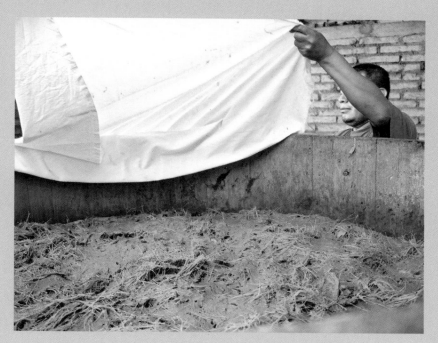

above: The crushed agaves are mixed with water in vats, covered, and left to ferment.

below: Without modern technologies, maestro mezcaleros like Vago's Aquilino García López smell, taste, and listen to the fermentation tanks to know when the batch is ready.

BUZZWORD: ORGANIC

Historically, traditional mezcal distilleries are lowercase-*o* "organic" by default. Agaves grow unpolluted in the wild, natural yeasts are used for fermentation, and the final products are left unadulterated. It's a natural, clean process. As the industry commercializes, however, some brands have sought formal certification for organic status in both Mexico and America. Regulations include (but are not limited to) paving concrete floors and creating proper ventilation in the distillation area and building barrier walls between the ovens and fermentation tanks to stop smoke overflow. For companies like Mezcales de Leyenda, Wahaka, Mezcal Amores, and Montelobos, certification is a way to prove they care about the organic nature of their liquid. For others, it's just one more hoop to jump through to satisfy the government. Many either don't have the funds required to follow guidelines, or choose not to in order to protect traditional methods of production. The bottom line is, if a label says certified organic, that's great! If not, that doesn't necessarily mean that the producer's processes aren't natural and respectable.

Another element that can be manipulated during fermentation is time. For most commercially produced spirits, fermentation takes roughly three days or so, depending on the climate and the kinds of yeast employed, but for mezcal, that number can vary. Why? In addition to accounting for climate and temperature, there's a personal choice involved. Even though the actual process of converting sugars into alcohol doesn't necessarily take weeks, the longer a mezcalero lets a batch evolve, the more layers of interesting flavor and aroma develop.

Jay Schroeder, former bar director for Mezcaleria Las Flores in Chicago, likens the process to making sour beer. "This is the cornerstone of why mezcal is so cool—the reason alone why I stopped drinking tequila altogether. I am a fan of bombastic statements by nature, but I mean that when I say it: Mezcal is the only spirit that has a long fermentation time beyond what is necessary," he said in a presentation on the spirit at Chicago's first Cocktail Summit in 2016. "It's like making a sour beer; we're building flavor and layering new aromas and flavors on top of our already complex source material. Imagine if you distilled a whiskey from a sour beer instead of ale. How much more flavor will be there? More acidity? Stranger aromas from that long fermentation?"

DISTILLATION

By this point, the fermented mash has become funky fresh and it's time to distill. At its most basic level, distillation is the process by which liquid—and in mezcal's case, sometimes fibers—are heated in a still so the liquid evaporates into a vapor and then condenses back into fluid again. And there you have it: hard liquor.

As with fermentation, the size, shape, and material of the vessel plays a role. Mezcaleros in rural areas use anything available. Copper pots are possibly the most commonly used vessels at established facilities and are sometimes preferred for their efficiency and neutral effect on flavor. Other regions, like Santa Catarina Minas in Oaxaca, are known for *minero*, or clay pot distillation. Not only is it more difficult and more expensive to distill in clay—the material often absorbs a percentage of each batch and the pots break easily and must be replaced frequently—but clay also influences the flavor. In expressions from Real Minero, Don Amado, and certain releases from Alipus and Siete Misterios, the spirit boasts a fuller body and a warm, earthy component, thanks to distillation *en barro*. Jake Lustig, owner of Don Amado, calls it a "briny" character. "Because we use small sixty-liter [sixteen-gallon] pot stills with lots

Mezcal distilleries where production goes back generations sometimes ferment in old, hollowed-out tree trunks, like this one at Mezcal Vago's Sola de Vega location.

above: Copper pots are often embedded in brick for temperature control. For the mezcal to qualify as artisanal or ancestral, the stills must be heated by fire.

opposite: Liquid trickles from the still at the Mezcal Vago palenque at Hacienda Tapanala.

previous pages: Copper pots might be the most common stills used in mezcal production.

of contact with distillate vapor, that essential soil quality is imparted into the mezcal," he says.

By law, mezcal must be distilled at least twice to an alcohol level between 36 and 55 percent. Companies like Wahaka Mezcal, Ilegal, Fidencio, El Buho, and Montelobos import at a lower 40 percent to appeal to what Americans are more comfortable drinking. Lowering the proof to a more palatable level can be helpful for the beginners, but it's sometimes a conflict among traditionalists. Historically, percentages have always landed on the higher end of the spectrum, a result not born from lawmaking but from preferred flavor profiles. "The alcohol level is really important," says Mezcaloteca co-owner Silvia Philion. "Only if you have 45 percent alcohol do you have enough alcohol to preserve the flavors and aromas. That's why mezcal at 40 percent feels pretty weak. Too much water and not enough alcohol."

Once the maestro has made the appropriate cuts and created the preferred balance, the liquid is bottled and readied for distribution.

top: Without modern technology, maestros often pour mezcal through a bamboo shoot and gauge ABV by the size of the resulting bubbles.

bottom: Maestros frequently check the liquid coming out of the still to determine when the desired ABV is achieved.

left: Tío Rey's palenque is a very small production—often it's just him running the show.

AGING

If you're a whiskey or brandy drinker, you probably understand that whiskey is aged in a barrel so that the product will taste better than it did the day before. The same rules don't really apply to mezcal. The liquid tastes expressive and interesting when it's au naturel, and about 95 percent of mezcal is released *joven*, or unaged, for this reason. Traditionalists, like the staff at Mezcaloteca in Oaxaca City, will reject aging or mark it as a sign of a bad mezcal, because the oak and vanilla tones of the wooden barrels are apt to mask the flavors of the spirit.

"Aging in wood barrels is a practice of the whiskey industry adopted into the world of tequila and mezcal to make it softer, but what really happens when you put a mezcal or tequila in a wood barrel is that you kill the finest flavors of the agave," says Silvia Philion. "If you like the flavors of the wood barrel you should

Aging is an uncommon practice in mezcal—oftentimes the flavors of the wood mask the natural personality of the liquid.

buy a whiskey, not a mezcal. In a mezcal you want to feel the flavor of the plant, the water, the woods in the process, the fermentation, et cetera."

On the flip side of that coin, there are companies and families making quality aged mezcal that's championed by barkeeps around the United States. Ilegal Mezcal was the first to market with a lineup of *joven*, *reposado*, and *añejo*. Other brands, like Don Amado and Los Amantes, also import aged expressions. "We have always used the Reposado con Gusano as a way to introduce tequila drinkers to mezcal," says Wahaka founder Alejandro Santa-Cruz. "Tequila drinkers are used to the reposados, and they are used to añejo and extra añejo, so it was a good way of teaching them that there's something beyond tequila, but it's still familiar."

Others are taking the experimentation even further. Mezcales de Leyenda toys with aging in different kinds of endemic wood to see how the local flair might

THE WORM

If you have poked around the world of mezcal at all, you've probably heard one of the many myths and hypotheses surrounding the inclusion of the worm (*gusano*) in the bottle. It will make you hallucinate! It's an aphrodisiac! Both are untrue. Historically, some say the little critter once represented high-quality mezcal—if the worm remained intact inside the liquid, the proof was high enough for preservation. Then, in the mid-1900s, the worm shifted from quality marker to gimmick as lesser-quality brands aimed to attract the attention of tourists and foreigners. Look, a worm! Aren't we cool? That trend continued for decades, and today it's near impossible to find a bottle of mezcal *con gusano* that is made in a quality way.

As usual, exceptions do exist, but they are few and far between. One that comes to mind is Wahaka Mezcal Reposado con Gusano, in which the worm was added for a singular reason: flavor. "The reposado is aged in an oak barrel, so it has vanilla flavor that's typical of oak, and the gusano adds an earthy, licorice, and bacon flavor," founder Alejandro Santa-Cruz says. "It's a recipe that our mezcalero's family has produced for fifty or sixty years, so I'm not one to go to maestro Alberto [Morales] and his great-grandfather and say, 'Hey that's not mezcal.' They've been producing that way for years and years, so it's traditional and continues to be one of our bestsellers."

mingle with the raw flavors. "My problem with aging mezcal is that they're following the whiskey and tequila tradition of these really smoky, charred, vanillin whiskey barrels that take over all of the flavor," says Mezcales de Leyenda partner Danny Mena. "It's not adding to the flavor of the mezcal, in my opinion. We're aiming to find something that adds flavors that make sense, and if it makes it better, that's great."

Wood barrels remain a subject of contention, but mezcal producers almost uniformly agree that letting mezcal spend time in glass produces fruitful results. "Maestros always used to store mezcal in glass bottles. Some would keep them underground for temperature control, and without light. Now, most of the mezcal we sell is young, just distilled, and that's not the best," says Philion. "When you leave it to rest in a neutral material like glass, a mix of many flavors comes to a balance." At Mezcaloteca, her Oaxacan mezcaleria, they feature a collection of old mezcales aged in glass, including a cultivated espadín from 1998. "Even though it's an espadín, it's so complex," Philion says. "As long as you serve your mezcal and seal it well again, it can be there for years and years and get better over time always, because it has a high alcohol [content]."

PECHUGA

It's Día de los Muertos in Santiago Matatlán, where the largest concentration of mezcal producers in Oaxaca clusters, and throughout the maze-like neighborhood fireworks pop and shriek, making me jump out of my skin as every nearby resident works to wake the dead.

Today I'm visiting the home of Asis Cortés, a vocal agave advocate and sixth-generation member of the family that produces Agave de Cortés and Jolgorio Mezcal. Near the edge of the courtyard, Cortés's mother is stirring a traditional chicken soup for breakfast, and his father, uncle, and grandfather sit around a table nearby discussing business. I'm stuffed at a table with a few dozen bartenders from every corner of the world, and the Bulgarian bar manager next to me won't stop cackling about his escapades the night before. A bottle of mezcal gets passed around before breakfast— and it's a *pechuga*, a distillate infused with meat (yes, meat) and made only for special occasions like today.

I can't help but let out a tiny groan. It's too early in the morning for all this

Pechuga is made by infusing mezcal with fruit, spices, or sometimes meat (including poultry) during distillation.

TRY THESE PECHUGAS

The differences between pechuga mezcals can be like night and day. Some burst with spice and fruit; others taste closer to the base spirit, with hints of savory roundness. In addition to the ones mentioned in the text already, here are a few more favorites.

REAL MINERO PECHUGA Distillation in clay pot stills gives this a round mouthfeel and fountainhead of depth. Made with chicken, pineapple, raisin, anise, plantains, and cinnamon, the 51.7 percent alcohol mezcal finishes long with warm flavors of ash and stone.

DON MATEO DE LA SIERRA PECHUGA Cenizo serves as the base agave varietal for this wily pechuga, made with deer and turkey. Distilled in a copper pot with pine and oyamel wood, it's light-bodied and fresh, with a clean, crazy minerality that bursts from the glass as a soft sweetness emerges, like cream cheese frosting. A real beauty, and great for beginners at 45 percent ABV.

VAGO ELOTE *Elote* isn't exactly the same as other pechugas in the sense that only a single ingredient meets the still during the infusion, but that addition makes such a gorgeous impact on the flavor, it's worth mentioning. Between the first and second distillations, a base of espadín is infused with corn grown on Aquilino García López's farm in Candelaria Yegolé, Oaxaca, contributing hints of earthy toasted corn, honeycomb, and mint to the glass. With a big, creamy body and a warming 50.6 percent ABV, it's a can't-miss.

opposite: Asis Cortés pours mezcal for guests at a Día de los Muertos celebration. Pechugas are often distilled and served expressly for special occasions.

THE CHEER IN MEZCAL IS *STIGIBEU*, AND IT MEANS, "TO YOUR HEALTH, TO THE HEALTH OF YOUR FRIENDS, AND THE LIFE OF MOTHER EARTH AND WITH GRATITUDE TO THE GODS THAT BROUGHT US AGAVE." IT'S REALLY RESPECTFUL; IT'S CONNECTED TO THE PLANET AND THE LIFE CYCLES OF THE PLANTS.

–RON COOPER, DEL MAGUEY

poultry, I think to myself. Why did we stay at In Situ so late the night before? I reluctantly take a sip, and every muscle relaxes. The Bulgarian's wily jokes fade into the background and I feel grounded again. The texture is soft and the savory notes subdued. I feel revitalized.

Think of pechuga as a sort of Mexican gin—a style of mezcal made by infusing fruits, spices, and sometimes meat during the second or third distillation to add new flavor different than those of the natural agave spirit alone. Meat sounds too wacky? While nightmares of poorly made bacon-infused bourbon and fat-washed martinis might be the first things to spring to mind, pechuga mezcal isn't gimmicky. The protein influence is subtle and the mezcals rarely (if ever) taste like actual meat. Instead of a smack of chicken breast on the palate, in most cases it's difficult for the layperson to identify specific proteins when tasting blind. *Pollo*, or chicken, is the most popular ingredient in Oaxaca, and other states and regions use venison, turkey, rabbit, or iguana to add an intriguing savory component.

Historically, pechugas were made only for celebrations and rituals, with the recipes handed down through the generations. "Mezcal pechuga was known before as a *Mezcal del Pecho del Mezcalero*, which means from the heart of the mezcalero," Cortés explains. "For a long time the mezcaleros would only make pechuga for special moments in their lives. That's how my grandfather wanted us to do it, so my dad and my uncle make it that way. We share a small part of the batch that day with the family and friends, and then we bottle the rest."

As the style has found commercial favor in the past decade or so, many producers have added a pechuga to their regular lineup or as a one-off release, simply using the style as a vehicle for creativity, like the Mezonte pechuga made in Michoacán with iguana and deer. The flavor is otherworldly, like rockets of minerality with deep cherry flavors and a touch of salinity on the finish. Mayalen's hyper-savory Borrego label has high basil notes and undercurrents of cinnamon from a lamb infusion, and Del Maguey won the Best New Spirit Award at Tales of the Cocktail in 2014 for their special edition Ibérico, a collaboration between Ron Cooper and Spanish chef José Andrés made with black-footed Iberian pigs fed on a diet of acorns.

Some still adhere to the seasonal framework, like the other pechuga from Del Maguey, a chicken-based recipe only made at the end of fall to capture the essence of apples and plums in season during that time. La Niña del Mezcal's pechuga—a solid introduction to the style—is made only in November by the Jimenez family in Santiago Matatlán. The recipe has been passed down through five generations and features turkey and pineapple, apple, guava, *tejocotes* (*manzanita*), and cinnamon. "Our pechuga has a tropical yet sweet flavor, reminiscent of a traditional Christmas punch that is served all over Mexico," says owner Cecilia Murrieta. "Most pechugas are seasonal, so depending on the type of year when it's produced, that's the flavors you'll get. I have a friend who makes them in April and May, and it's super citrusy with lots of fresh grapefruit, lime, orange peels."

For the vegan crowd, producers like Cinco Sentidos and Wahaka take the meat out of the equation with certain releases. The former's mole pechuga brings a warm, chocolatey blast of regional cuisine to the bottle, and the latter boasts vivid fruit flavors in the nanche- and apple-fueled varieties. Just be ready to spend a pretty penny to explore the category. Because *mezcal de pechuga* is special and requires additional ingredients, bottles tend to tip towards the higher end of the spectrum—around fifty dollars up to one hundred fifty and more.

PART THREE

IN THE GLASS

First, it's good to note that historically, mezcal is consumed neat. No ice. No water. No bullshit. It's one of the few spirits in the world where the raw material has so much flavor that you don't have to do anything to it to enjoy what's in the glass.

"We have the motto 'Sip it, don't shoot it,'" Del Maguey's Ron Cooper says. It's a catchphrase woven into the consciousness of bartenders and consumers everywhere, and for good reason—in some ways, the mantra was necessary in the early days to differentiate mezcal from tequila's rowdy "spring break" image. "Tequila has been industrialized. It's watered down," Cooper says. "Tequila culture is mariachis and cowboys, and slamming shots. Good mezcal is like sipping culture."

On a more practical side, mezcal is often much higher proof than bourbon, gin, or vodka. When you get into a range of 45 to 100 percent alcohol by volume, "intense" becomes something of an understatement. Shooting liquor at such high proofs will knock you on your ass faster than you could say "Cheers" in Zapotec—*dixeebe*!

To ease in, Cooper suggests warming up the palate before tasting for flavors. "The very first sip, you have to squeeze your tongue up into the roof of your mouth and teeth and swallow slowly. After that first intense sip, you wait thirty seconds and your palate is tuned up and you can sip normally. The second sip is sweeter and softer. It changes."

opposite: Because mezcal is often higher proof than other spirits, it's wise to sip instead of shoot.

113

Jason Cox pours a flight at El Destilado in Oaxaca City.

FINDING THE RIGHT MEZCAL

By now hopefully you realize there's so much diversity in the category, you could try different expressions for the rest of your life and probably still discover a new flavor every day. It's incredibly exciting. On the other hand, that same breadth of diversity can be one of the spirit's most intimidating aspects. Whether at the bar or liquor store, facing down dozens of bottles can be confusing at best. Each one coming from a different producer or region, using different agave plants, and adding its own twists on the production process. Where to start? How do you figure out which agave will speak to you? With high price points and without any guidance, the process can be a gamble.

   One of the best ways to get to know the spirit is to find a bartender you trust at a place with a healthy mezcal selection and let them guide you through the journey. Chances are, they've done the research and have put in countless hours tasting through each brand and variety already, meaning they'll be able to quickly and easily help you find a good match. But, if you're a stubborn independent (like I am), here are a few suggestions for navigating the waters of mezcal on your own.

LINE UP A FLIGHT

When getting to know mezcal, it's smart to taste through as much as you can, as often as you can. The first time I tasted mezcal, the only thing I noticed was the smoke. Now, I get a full symphony of flavors and personalities with each sip. Flights are great because you can easily compare and contrast brands without investing in an entire bottle. Here are some ways modern mezcalerias organize flight options.

BY VARIETY

Organize a few samples from the same species to get a loose sense for a certain style. Start with espadín—the most widely available (and more affordable) variety. As more rare agaves hit the market, some folks are starting to think of espadín as the boring option, but that's jumping the gun. Just because it's ubiquitous doesn't mean it's dull. Mezcal El Silencio's espadín tastes sweeter and fruitier than the espadín from Mezcal Koch, for example. Both are delicious, for different reasons. Pierde Almas's espadín comes out swinging with big, boisterous character, while Alipus tends toward the more modest end of the spectrum. Once you get a good baseline on espadín, it doesn't hurt to get a little wild, if the pocketbook allows. Try a few pours from the *karwinskii* family, like cuishe, madre-cuishe, bicuixe, or largo.

BY TERROIR

Elevation, soil type, microclimate, and other elements of terroir also arguably make an impact on the flavor of mezcal, so it's interesting to consider where and when the plants were grown when thinking in terms of flavor. Was the soil full of nutrients, or did the agave struggle for most of its growth? Altitude is

> GETTING TO KNOW MEZCAL IS LIKE GETTING TO KNOW DIFFERENT PEOPLE AND DECIDING IF YOU LIKE THEM OR NOT. THAT'S THE MAIN THING ABOUT MEZCAL—YOU HAVE A LOT OF TRADITION AND BACKGROUND FOR EACH ONE, SO IT'S A UNIVERSE OF DIFFERENT FLAVORS. IT'S A BEAUTIFUL THING.
>
> —PEDRO JIMÉNEZ, PARE DE SUFRIR

above: At La Botica in Mexico City, the menu is organized by region so you can compare and contrast differences in mezcals geographically.

opposite: At El Destilado in Oaxaca City, modern Oaxacan food is meant to pair with the house mezcal.

important, because different yeast strains live at different elevations, and each imparts its own special flavor personality during fermentation. Again, sweeping statements can't be made in terms of exactly what you're going to taste, but knowing terroir can spark interesting new insights and conversations.

At Espita Mezcaleria in Washington, D.C., beverage director Josh Phillips lines up a flight of Nuestra Soledad to best highlight this concept. Try the 2014 espadín from the village of Lachigui, the 2015 from Santiago Matatlán, and the 2014 made in Zoquitlán—all espadín mezcals from various parts of Oaxaca, with different regional peculiarities. "We choose these three because they are all fairly traditional espadín flavor profiles and we wanted to show that even within the 'expected' flavors there is still a huge range of flavors represented," he says. Look for light smoke and papaya from the Lachigui, orange peel and caramel from the Santiago Matatlán, and ancho and worn leather characteristics from the Santa Maria Zoquitlán bottling.

BY REGION

In addition to differences in soil and terroir, traditions and tools differ by region as well, which can also impact flavor. In the case of Santa Catarina Minas—a pueblo located just outside of Oaxaca City with a subtropical microclimate—almost all producers use clay pot stills, which creates a round, earthy flavor in a mezcal. Try three pours from Santa Catarina Minas, such as Real Minero Espadín, Don Amado Rústico, and Del Maguey Minero.

> MEZCAL IS JUST LIKE WINE. YOU HAVE ALL OF THESE SPECIES, AND DIFFERENT VARIETIES FROM DIFFERENT AREAS HAVE DIFFERENT QUALITIES. YOU CAN DRINK A MEZCAL THAT'S FLORAL AND BRIGHT WITH CARAMEL NOTES AND THEN DRINK ANOTHER ONE THAT'S DRY AND ASHY. THE COMPLEXITY OF FLAVOR IS ASTOUNDING.
>
> –KEHLEN SELPH,
> THE PASTRY WAR, HOUSTON

HAND OF THE MAKER

Get to know the hand of the maker and the philosophy of the distiller by investigating the different mezcaleros who produce under a certain label. Order Vago espadín en barro or tobalá made by mezcalero Salomón Rey Rodriguez, and then try a few from Aquilino García López, like the Elote or mexicano. The differences might be subtle, but if you pay close enough attention, you might notice that a certain elegance weaves throughout Aquilino's light-bodied mezcals, while Tío Rey's tend to have a bigger body with more savory and mineral flavors.

Veladoras, or old candleholders, are the most common vessel used for serving mezcal across Mexico.

Del Maguey makes terracotta *copitas* for sipping. One of the only brand-specific drinking vessels out there, it's also one of the most widely found mezcal-specific drinking cups in the US.

GLASSWARE

Coming from an American perspective, I always thought those ubiquitous clay drinking cups were the only way people drank mezcal. Turns out, there's a wide variety of options out there, some more traditional than others. To see which experience you like best, try a few of these on for size.

JÍCARA

Born out of necessity during the early days of mezcal production, the rugged-looking *jícara* is actually half of a hollowed-out gourd. Thanks to its oval shape and shallow depth, mezcal rests neatly in the bottom while the aromas float freely into the air. Jícaras add a rustic feel to a nip of mezcal, but they do have downsides: they're almost impossible to clean (soap residue often clings to the inside) and they aren't easy to rest on a table due to the curved base.

VELADORA

A cross marks the bottom of all *vaso veladoras*, revealing the cups' original purpose as containers for prayer candles in Catholic churches across Mexico. Centuries ago, the glasses were repurposed for drinking mezcal and are now found abundantly in mezcalerias and restaurants around Mexico. While they look a bit like wide, ribbed shot glasses, the key to the veladora is the broad mouth, which allows aromas to circulate better. A popular saying in Oaxaca is *Hasta que ver la cruz*, meaning "Drink until you see the cross."

COPITA

There's something grounding about sipping mezcal from a clay *copita* (opposite). One of the only brand-specific drinking vessels out there, the tiny terracotta drinking cups are made exclusively by Del Maguey. Ron Cooper aimed to create a shape that would allow for the aromas of mezcal to emanate while honoring Zapotec tradition with the selection of material. Cooper has worked with the same family in Oaxaca for the last twenty-one years and has given out thousands of free copitas to bars and bartenders. With sets now available online, it's one of the most widely found mezcal-specific drinking cups in the United States.

WINE GLASS

Many contemporary producers say glass is the best vessel for drinking mezcal, as it provides a neutral palate for delivering aromas and flavors. With stem or without is a matter of personal preference, but as with wine, the ability to swish and swirl the mezcal feels pleasant and helps agitate the volatile aromas.

WORM SALTS AND ORANGE SLICES

Remember the worm discussed in Part Two? The little critter plays another key role in the narrative of mezcal—this time, outside of the bottle. As an ingredient, the *gusano* has served as a culinary delicacy since pre-Hispanic times, originally reserved for the wealthy and powerful (think Aztec emperors). The crunchy insects remained deeply intertwined in Mexican culinary tradition, along with other bugs like *chapulínes* (grasshoppers) and *escamoles* (ant larvae), bringing depth to quesadillas and tamales, seasoning salsas and meats, and adding texture to bar snacks. The red worm is also dried, toasted, and ground into one of mezcal's most common side condiments: *sal de gusano*, or worm salt.

"The tradition of the worm salt is almost as old as mezcal itself," says Diana Corona, who makes a zesty blend under the Gran Mitla label distributed into the US via a partnership with Mezcal Vago. "When mezcal was ready to drink, some people used to taste it with salt sprinkled on an orange slice," she explains. "Soon they found that the worm's intense agave taste was a perfect match and started to grind dried worms with salt and pepper."

Savory sal de gusano has a barbecue-like flavor that oozes umami and is almost always served alongside mezcal, sprinkled on top of (or served in a tiny pile alongside) orange slices. There's no specific ritual to follow in terms of how to consume it from that point, but some encourage using the slices and salt as a palate cleanser between sips. "The red agave worm is very smoky, so it complements the earthy flavors of the mezcal," says Monica Martinez, owner of Don Bugito, an edible insect company based in San Francisco. "The sweetness of the orange helps balance those flavors."

Until recently, the condiment was almost impossible to find in the States, but options are expanding as mezcal producers (and some independent companies like Don Bugito) start exporting vials. Ingredients typically stay the same—salt, dried and crushed chili peppers, and toasted worms—but types of chili pepper, grade of salt, and ratio of crushed insects varies by region and producer, meaning a pleasing diversity can be found within the category. The level of grind also shifts, with companies like Sal de Aquí opting for a medium-level grind, while Gran Mitla and Marca Negra make coarse, chunky blends, as does the crew behind Mezcal Pierde Almas, though their product isn't formally distributed. Instead, owner Jonathan Barbieri saves their salt for special occasions and gifts and ships a percentage up to New York every year to accompany dishes like octopus tostada, burrata quesadilla, and toro taquitos at Julian Medina's restaurants Toloache and Tacuba.

GREAT WORM SALTS TO SEEK OUT

Worm salt is the perfect umami accompaniment to a glass of mezcal, but the cost of a bottle can sometimes cause a jolt of sticker shock, with prices ranging from $15 to over $200, depending on size. Don Bugito's Monica Martinez explains, "Red agave worm is actually very expensive because it's a lot of physical labor to remove it from the plant, and it only happens once a year." Price tag aside, seek out one of these delicious brands for maximum enjoyment.

Orange slices are the traditional accompaniment to mezcal, but some bars and brands are thinking outside the box and offering other fruits and salts to complement the various flavors of the liquid.

above: Worm salt is either sprinkled directly on top of orange wedges or served in a pile on the side so you can adjust according to preference.

opposite: Worm salt is the perfect complement to a sip of mezcal.

Bitterman Salt Co.: Made with pasilla and arbol chilies, hand-harvested Oaxacan sea salt, and worms, this sal de gusano comes from the Portland, Oregon, company responsible for an array of popular culinary salts. Purchase via the Meadow (www.themeadow.com).

Don Bugito: This San Francisco business was one of the first in the United States to focus on the allure of edible insects, so it's natural that they would create a salt with gusano. Made with two kinds of chili pepper and worms imported from an agave farm in San Luis Potosí, their sal de gusano can be purchased online (www.donbugito.com), or found in bars such as Espita Mezcaleria in Washington, D.C., Two James Spirits in Detroit, and Calavera in Oakland.

Gran Mitla: Sourcing from Oaxaca but officially based in Mexico City, Gran Mitla comes to the United States in partnership with Mezcal Vago. The company makes two kinds of super-chunky salt meant for tasting alongside mezcal: traditional sal de gusano made with sea salt, toasted red agave worms, and four types of chili pepper, as well as a nutty chapulíne salt made with grasshoppers, salt, lime, and chilies. Buy a bottle (or a kilo) on their website (www. granmitla.us) or online from Specs (www.specsonline.com) or K&L Wines (www.klwines.com).

Marca Negra: Also opting for a relatively gritty texture, Marca Negra's sal de gusano (www.blackmarkbrands.com) is made with a type of rare chili native to Oaxaca called *Mixe*. Jars are sold primarily online through Amazon, though you might be lucky to find a bottle or two at liquor stores that carry the mezcal.

Sal de Aquí: A double hit of sal de gusano and sal de chapulínes anchor Sal de Aquí's line (www.saldeaqui.com.mx), but they also have a citrus and *xoconostle* (prickly pear) salt that pairs well with fresh fruits, salads, and cocktails. Available online and in markets across Mexico (and a few beyond).

Compania de Sales: Boasting an exciting contemporary line, Mezcal Sabios de Lua's sister outfit (www.companiadesales.com) imports modern flavors like gusano with *hoja santa* (a popular Mexican aromatic herb) and grasshopper with ginger.

AT THE TABLE

Some purists demand mezcal be sipped and savored without distraction—as an apéritif before dinner, or perhaps a digestive after—in order to experience and appreciate the spirit's soul in its unadulterated state. James Beard Award–winning chef Rick Bayless is one of these devotees. "Mezcal opens your palate, so you really want your *mezcalito* before you have your meal," he says. "At the end of the meal you put another bottle on the table, but it's not something you consume with food. Everybody wants to do these pairing dinners, but I can't stand them. You can taste a little mezcal with a dish and say, 'Oh, this goes well,' but do you really want to have a whole glass of it with your meal? I don't know if you do. It's just not my thing."

Among nontraditionalists, experimentation can be found on both sides of the border. Bar snacks like pickled veggies, fried fava beans, salty Marcona almonds, or sunflower seeds sprinkled with chapulínes help keep the wolves at bay, and as Bayless mentioned, pairing dinners are becoming increasingly popular as a means of introducing people to the spirit, with brands like Del Maguey, La Niña del Mezcal, and Pierde Almas hosting events at Tales of the Cocktail and beyond.

At other respectable restaurants like Julian Medina's Toloache Bistro Mexicano and Tacuba Cantina Mexciana in New York and *Top Chef México* winner Rodolfo Castellanos's Origen in Oaxaca, chefs and beverage directors work together to match mezcal with Mexican cuisine. Medina says, "The best pairing is with something rich and spicy like a good mole, a meaty braised short rib, or a simple duck à l'orange." Castellano prefers desserts. "You can be surprised at how well they go with chocolate," he says.

Danny Mena, chef at Hecho en Dumbo in New York City and partner in Mezcales de Leyenda favors a good chocolate pairing too. At a special dinner at Chicago's Masa Azul back in 2015, Mena introduced a decadent Mexican chocolate mousse with mezcal-lavender cream for dessert, paired with Leyenda's mezcal from Durango. The bitter orange peel, baked apple, and volcanic soil flavors of the mezcal melted into the chocolate with harmony. "Mezcal is an amazing digestif. The acidity cuts through high chocolatey, fatty desserts," he says. "It is often overlooked, but a good flan with our Durango is pretty magical."

Queso fundido is a common bar snack in Mexico and a delicious accompaniment to a veladora of mezcal.

At Mezcalito, an upscale bar and restaurant in the Russian Hill neighborhood of San Francisco, El Destilado chef Julio Aguilera helped executive chef Matt D'Ambrosi design a menu around food and mezcal pairings. Dishes like the smoky oyster mignonette explode with salinity when paired with a mineral-driven espadín like the Doba-Yej from Siete Misterios, and the bar's charred peanut sauce slathered over octopus tostadas reaches new depths of complexity when paired with the nutty, chocolate notes of Rey Campero Cuishe.

"Every restaurant that's well respected in Mexico is pairing mezcal with food," Mezcalito beverage director Guadalupe Jaques says. "I had an eighteen-course meal at [El Destilado] with a mezcal pairing for almost everything. [Beverage director Jason Cox] is pairing Papalome fermented in rawhide with steak—that rawhide comes through so you taste the leather and gaminess together. He's pairing mole with a mole pechuga from Puebla. It's awesome."

At El Destilado, the philosophy behind food pairings is carefully planned, with course after course matched based on the minerality, smokiness, and vegetal flavors of mezcal and how each might complement or contrast with the restaurant's modern but distinctly Oaxacan cuisine. Jason Cox explains, "At this point we have a really good register of the flavors of our different courses. We also have a good idea of the tasting notes you'll find in mezcal." His only word of advice? Don't pair mezcal with spicy foods, because it can amp the spice level out of control.

"People who don't pair mezcal with food probably just don't know how to do it yet," Jaques says. His only concern is seeing people force the issue. "I haven't seen enough people do it successfully, so I think that having the first-person experience doing it with Jason helped me expand my mind. There's so much complexity there, you should be able to do things of that nature."

Cox agrees. "We'll definitely start to see more and more people doing pairings with mezcal to introduce people to the spirit," he says, "but it shouldn't be forced. If it doesn't make sense, don't do it."

opposite: Dishes like the ceviche at El Destilado make a bright match for this complex ensamble from Cinco Sentidos.

following pages: Mezcal is high proof—it's wise to line the stomach with bar snacks for fortification.

PART FOUR

MEZCAL COCKTAILS

The success of mezcal [in the US] was driven by the craft cocktail movement, because it was the bartenders who were interested in mezcal; they had a palate that was developed enough to understand the complex nuances of the spirit.

—Misty Kalkofen, Del Maguey

When Del Maguey's Misty Kalkofen takes groups of eager bartenders on educational visits to the company's palenques in Oaxaca, she often asks everyone to bring a prepared bottled cocktail for the mezcaleros. "Sometimes they don't really understand why we're selling so much, and why each year the quantity we're purchasing from them is going up. So it's really fun for them to see how the bartenders are using it," she says.

Nine times out of ten, she says, the mezcalero will taste the cocktail and be very respectful about the whole scenario. But when asked which drink they prefer, most usually smile politely and point to the mezcal.

I don't blame them, but if I had a dollar for every time a mezcal purist has looked at me with a pained grimace when I admit to enjoying mezcal cocktails, I could stock my entire bar with rare and wild bottles. Many traditionalists say

opposite: Bartender Anne Vaughn mixes up a Last Word at Whisler's in Austin, Texas.

that by mixing with mezcal you're missing the point. In his book *Mezcalaria: The Cult of Mezcal*, In Situ Mezcaleria owner Ulises Torrentera calls mixology "the fanciest manner to degrade mezcal." He continues, "Cocktails are for unrefined tastes that require other elements to cloak the strong, and at the same time soft, flavor of mezcal. Nonetheless, in the present day they are all the rage. And mixologists are inventing new cocktails that while they do taste nicely, they are in a way hiding the essence of mezcal."

It's a perspective that might sound aggressively one-sided, but to be fair, this dogmatic approach does have some merit. To really understand and appreciate mezcal's dazzling array of complex flavors and aromas, the pathway is straightforward: drink it neat. On the flip side, you can't talk about the spirit's rise (in America, anyway) without acknowledging the role of the cocktail. Not only is the spirit incredibly versatile when combined with other ingredients; its use in cocktails has galvanized the growth of the category and continues to be the reason why so many new agave lovers are born.

"One smell and I thought, 'Holy shit, what is this? I've never tasted anything like this,'" Kalkofen says, recalling her introduction to the spirit back in 2008. Ron Cooper had brought a few bottles of pechuga and tobalá to Cambridge, Massachusetts, bar and restaurant Green Street, where she was closing the bar that night. Her instinct was to start shaking. "[Mezcal varieties] are all so different from one another. Imagine, the exact same cocktail recipe with five different mezcals—you're going to get five remarkably different drinks. There's no way you can just substitute a different one in and have the same effect. That was really exciting to me, and it was the same for all these other bartenders."

Motivated by the possibilities, she added a number of mezcal drinks to the menu at Green Street before leaving to helm the program at Drink cocktail bar in Boston a year later. There she popularized mezcal cocktails like her Zocalo, a martini-like mix with cinnamon syrup, mezcal, orange bitters, and dry vermouth. Like wildfire, the spirit started to spread. Also in 2009, Anvil Bar & Refuge opened in Houston, Texas, with the Brave cocktail (page 185) on the menu, and bartenders like Alex Day, Brian Miller, and Phil Ward were experimenting

> # THE COCKTAIL IS THE INTRODUCTION, RIGHT? IT SPARKS THAT LIGHT OF CURIOSITY THAT GETS PEOPLE TO WANT TO TRY THAT MEZCAL.
>
> **–GUADALUPE JAQUES, MEZCALITO, SAN FRANCISCO**

El Destilado bartender Carlos Martinez Guzmán pours one of the house cocktails.

with the spirit at Death & Co. in New York. Ward left to open what has since become the most notable agave bar in the country, Mayahuel.

The mezcaleria-like bar opened with a focus on tequila but quickly became home to a substantial lineup of Del Maguey bottles. On the opening menu, drinks like the Division Bell (page 160), Lip Spin #2 (page 189), and Oaxaca Old Fashioned (page 182) drew further attention to the spirit. In the latter, a split pour of tequila and mezcal anchors Ward's riff on the Old Fashioned, and with agave nectar instead of sugar, the spin is often cited as the first drink to spark the viability of mezcal in a cocktail framework.

Around this time, journalists began praising the mezcal cocktail too, with headlines in the *New York Times*, the *Wall Street Journal*, *Food and Wine*, *Saveur*, and *Imbibe*. In a 2011 *Food Republic* story on bartender Joaquín Simó's Naked and Famous cocktail, bartender Naren Young waxed poetic about the format: "While I encourage you to sip your heart out, the entire category is being driven by its use in cocktails, especially in New York, where this mezcal revolution began. Sipping a great mezcal is a beautiful thing, but now almost every cocktail menu at every decent cocktail bar has at least one mezcal drink proudly on it."

above: Some bars, like Ghost Donkey in New York, the Pastry War in Houston, and Mezcaleria Las Flores in Chicago, pair mezcal with other traditional Mexican ingredients in their cocktails.

opposite: While some purists may turn up their noses at the notion of sullying mezcal's complexities via mixing, it is those very complexities that make mezcal ideal for cocktails.

Today, the spirit has come even further in the cocktail world, with places like Mezcaleria Las Flores in Chicago and Houston's the Pastry War designing drinks within a cultural framework to bring attention to the spirit's roots. In Houston, recipes like Kehlen Selph's Age of Discovery (page 194) are bestsellers, proving that mezcal has come a long way from the margarita and the Old Fashioned. "Everything we do at the Pastry War has to be culturally significant to Mexico," Selph says. "Just because a cocktail has tequila or mezcal doesn't mean it's Mexican. I tell my staff and myself to find inspiration in ingredients in food, other cocktails, or alcohol-free beverages, candies, or desserts in Mexico. They'll usually pair really well with mezcal because they all come from the same background."

Now that mezcal cocktails can be found on bar menus throughout the States, the trend is trickling back down to the other side of the border, where bartenders are throwing mezcal into a shaker tin to see what comes out. "Guess what's growing in Oaxaca? The craft cocktail movement!" Kalkofen says.

MODIFIERS
TO KNOW

XTABENTÚN This slightly floral, deeply herbaceous liqueur from the Yucatán region of Mexico is made with anise and honey. Bottles can be tricky to find, but the results—a subtle depth and crisp twinge of licorice-like flavor in drinks like the Texecutioner (page 147)—make the hunt worthwhile.

ANCHO REYES Montelobos Mezcal's sister company makes this liqueur from dried ancho peppers sourced from Puebla. Naturally, it goes best with agave spirits. It's spicy, slightly smoky, and adds toothsome depth to cocktails like the Jamaicón (page 167). The newest expression to market, Verde, is made with green poblano peppers and brings a verdant punch to the Michelada (page 217).

BITTERMENS HELLFIRE HABANERO SHRUB Taking inspiration from the vinegary goodness of hot sauce, Bittermens invented this shrub (a kind of historic fruit- and vinegar-based syrup) to bring a blast of fiery heat to the glass. It packs a heavyweight punch—just a few drops will add a piquant habanero flavor that'll offset sweetness in drinks like the Ready Fire Aim (page 151) and Clever Club (page 163).

Bitters line the shelf at El Destilado in Oaxaca City.

HERBOLARIA
BITTERS
· SACRIS GUSTUS ·

MOLE OAXAQUEÑO

Hand Crafted | No2 | Lote:

120 ML / 4oz

CHAPPYS BITTERS

CHERRY

"Every time I'm down there, I'm invited to do seminars and guest bartending nights to talk about how to use mezcal in cocktails and stuff like that. The cocktail scene in Mexico City is exploding too, and it's super cool."

In Mexico's capital city, gin and rum are still more commonly found on cocktail menus, but at places like Limantour—a chic joint in the Roma Norte neighborhood named one of the World's 50 Best Bars in 2016—the tides are starting to turn. There, an eclectic menu features a few mezcal gems, including the Mezcal Stalk (page 159), a simple mix of pineapple juice, triple sec, and

Thanks to its robust, punchy personality, mezcal plays well with other strong-willed spirits and flavors, like Amari, rum, and whiskey.

Cocktails are a great introduction to mezcal for beginners.

mezcal, and the Vicuña, made with *Agave cupreata* mezcal, smoked pineapple juice, Chilean pisco, lemon juice, and agave nectar. In both drinks, the mezcal shines through instead of getting lost in the static of too many ingredients. "People in Mexico are getting very interested in mezcal cocktails," says bar director José Luis León Martinez. "It is incredible to see how bartenders are playing with this product that for years was considered the alcohol for poor people. Now it's a kind of pride for us—to have this product in our shakers, and try to show to the world how to use it, how to enjoy it, and how to love it."

The sentiment echoes in Oaxaca City, where it's now easy to find mezcal added to a variety of *refrescos* at restaurants like Expendio Tradicion, Origen, and Criollo. At Sabina Sabe, a modern spot near the Zocalo run by head bartender Alfredo Corro Enríquez, the cocktail program skews more contemporary, with some recognizable classics and others with more pizazz. "Today we find Negronis, Sazeracs, mezcal tonics, mojitos, and margaritas made with mezcal inside and outside of Mexico," says Corro. At Sabina Sabe, his approach is to keep things as uncomplicated as possible, like in the Jamaicón (page 167), with fresh hibiscus and chili peppers, and the Guayabo Verde, in which Chartreuse adds an herbaceous bite to the refreshing flavors of guava and tonic water. "I think this gives us a clear picture of the contribution of mezcal. Its earthy flavor goes well with serious, fresh, tropical drinks, and its smoky highlights give a plus to boozy, stirred ones."

MAESTRO MEZCALERO ..... Miguel Angel Partida Rivera

ESTADO ..... Jalisco

COMUNIDAD ..... Zapotitlan de Vadillo

MAGUEY(ES) EMPLEADO(S) ..... A. Rhughaianthe H. Angustifolia

EDAD DE MAGUEY ..... 12, 10, 7, 6 años

TIPO DE HORNO ..... Tierra Alineado con Piedra

TIPO DE LEÑA ..... Mezquite

TIEMPO DE COCCIÓN ..... 72 horas

TONELADAS HORNEADAS .....

TIPO DE MOLIDO ..... Manual c/ machas de madera

TINA DE FERMENTACIÓN ..... Robble Plastico

TIPO DE AGUA ..... Manantial

TIEMPO DE FERMENTACIÓN .....

AT HOME

In the following pages, you'll find a slew of cocktails made from smart bartenders around the US and Mexico. Some recipes are bona fide icons that should be recognized for their role in boosting mezcal's popularity, like the Oaxaca Old Fashioned (page 182), Single Village Fix (page 178), and Ready Fire Aim (page 151). Others have deeper cultural roots, like the Raicilla Batanga (page 208), the Champurrado (page 223), and the Age of Discovery (page 194). The section is organized by style—drinks with citrus get shaken; those with only spirits and modifiers are stirred; and highballs have soda or a sparkling element to freshen up the palate. A few oddballs, like the coffee-punctuated Espumita Blanca (page 224) and the frozen Pinche Fresas (page 225) are tossed in to keep things lighthearted.

If you're new to mezcal, the best place to start is by tracing the same trajectory bartenders have followed and begin with the classics. Take something familiar like the margarita (page 148), Paloma (page 214), Negroni (page 181) or Old Fashioned (page 182) and see how mezcal transforms those comfortable flavors into something multidimensional.

As far as what to mix with, almost all cocktails star espadín. Flavor-wise, it's a consistent style that produces relatively predictable effects when fused with other ingredients, which is a bonus when it comes to cocktails. Del Maguey Vida is still the most frequently used expression in the States, but others also have good mixability and great price points, like Banhez, a sweeter espadín-barril blend, the even-keeled Montelobos, soulful Wahaka Joven, and muscular Vago espadín. Recipes like the Mayor Rock (page 193) and Oakland (page 197) feature varieties that are slightly less common, and I like to consider those reserved for special occasions. Just as you might not incorporate that expensive bottle of Scotch into a Blood and Sand, I'm not throwing back tobalá and arroqueño cocktails every night.

Speaking from one home bartender to (likely) another, heed my advice and don't stray too far outside of the recommended brands. Bartenders go to great lengths to find the perfect matches for each ingredient to make the drink sing. Bottles like Amari and vermouth can vary far more than one might suspect, so by staying true to their recipes, you'll come out with the best-tasting results.

opposite: The mark of a quality mezcal is often its label. When stocking your bar, check for detailed information about how the product was made.

THE RECIPES

FRESH

SHAKEN, EASYGOING CITRUS- AND FRUIT-FORWARD DRINKS

TEXECUTIONER
EQUAL PARTS BRIGHT AROMATICS AND HERBACEOUS DEPTH

Cheekily named after Texas politician Rick Perry, Wahaka's brazen espadín serves as an herbal fortitude for this memorable mix. Crafted in 2011 by bartender Houston Eaves during his time at ranch-like restaurant Contigo in Austin, the recipe traveled down to San Antonio's historic Esquire Tavern after he relocated to Alamo City a year later. Thanks to its savvy balance of snappy grapefruit and sweet Cocchi Americano, the drink has endured as a menu staple at both bars. Drink it served up (as they do at Contigo) or on a large ice cube (as they do at Esquire), and watch for the punchy mezcal to soften as the honeysuckle and orange notes of Cocchi weave throughout.

- ¾ **OUNCE** Wahaka Espadín mezcal
- ¾ **OUNCE** Xtabentún
- ¾ **OUNCE** Cocchi Aperitivo Americano
- ¾ **OUNCE** fresh grapefruit juice
- **GRAPEFRUIT TWIST,** for garnish

Combine all ingredients in a shaker tin with ice and shake well. Strain into a coupe glass. Express the oil from a grapefruit swath over the top of the drink for aromatics, and garnish with grapefruit twist.

Houston Eaves, Esquire Tavern, San Antonio

MEZCAL MARGARITA

SIMPLE, BEAUTIFUL, TIMELESS

Three ingredients. Mezcal. Lime. Agave. Whether you sip on the rocks, up, or frozen, the margarita is the perfect introduction to how seamlessly mezcal works in cocktails. I prefer to let tequila and mezcal share real estate in the glass for extra complexity, but there's also something admirable about two solid ounces of mezcal. That's the approach at Empellon, where the Mezcal Margarita has been on the menu since the taqueria first opened in New York City in 2011. Beverage director Noah Small took inspiration from the grandfather of all tequila cocktails—the margarita at Tommy's in San Francisco—when coming up with the recipe. Effortless and refreshing.

2 OUNCES Del Amigo mezcal

1 OUNCE fresh lime juice

¾ OUNCE diluted agave syrup

Rim a rocks glass with salt (Empellon uses smoked salt) and set aside. Combine all ingredients in a shaker tin with ice. Shake until chilled and strain into the prepared rocks glass over fresh ice cubes.

For the diluted agave syrup, combine one part light agave nectar with one part hot water. Shake until both are combined. Let chill before using in a drink. Store in the refrigerator.

Noah Small, Empellon, New York City

READY FIRE AIM
A HINT OF HEAT ELEVATES THIS PINEAPPLE-DRIVEN TIPPLE

Many modern classics have emerged from the talented crew at Employees Only, so it's no surprise that one of the bar's earliest mezcal cocktails, the Ready Fire Aim, quickly secured legendary status after Steve Schneider designed the drink in 2013. With a memorable balance of sweet pineapple, mezcal, and a spark of habanero, the recipe has landed on menus all over the world, including EO's newest location in Singapore.

1¾ OUNCES Del Maguey Vida mezcal

1 OUNCE honey-pineapple syrup

¾ OUNCE pineapple juice

½ OUNCE fresh lime juice

3 DASHES Bittermens Hellfire Habanero Shrub

PINK PEPPERCORNS, for garnish

Combine ingredients in a shaker tin with ice. Shake until chilled and strain into a cocktail coupe. Sprinkle a small amount of pink peppercorn on top of the drink.

For the honey-pineapple syrup, combine 1 whole cubed pineapple with 50 pink peppercorns and set aside. Add 2 cups honey with 1 cup water to the vessel. Let sit overnight so the flavors combine. Strain into a clean container with a lid and store in the refrigerator for use.

Steve Schneider, Employees Only, New York City

SAFFRON

AN EARTHY TAKE ON THE TROPICAL JUNGLE BIRD

A pineapple- and saffron-flavored macaron served as the inspiration for this West Coast gem, and when bar owner Kevin Diedrich added mezcal, the connections clicked. Echoing the pinpoint-perfect bitter and sweet contrast of the Jungle Bird, a favorite from the realm of tiki cocktails, the ingredients merge together harmoniously for a vibrant tropical treat. I mix this one up in double batches, because I inevitably always want more than one round.

- **1½ OUNCES** saffron-infused Montelobos mezcal
- **1½ OUNCES** grilled pineapple juice
- **¾ OUNCE** Campari
- **½ OUNCE** fresh lime juice
- **½ OUNCE** agave nectar
- **2 PINEAPPLE** leaves, for garnish
- **CHARRED PINEAPPLE** core wedge, for garnish

Shake ingredients together in a shaker tin with ice. Double-strain into a footed sour glass over fresh ice. Garnish with pineapple leaf and pineapple core with grilled edge.

For the grilled pineapple juice, peel and cut one whole pineapple around the core. Save leaves for garnish. Grill pineapple until it has grill marks and starts to darken. Grill core as well and set to the side to use for garnish later. Juice grilled pineapple and fine-strain pulp out of the liquid. Cut grilled core into cubes to be used as garnish.

For the saffron-infused mezcal, add 1 tablespoon saffron threads to 1 liter mezcal and let steep for 2 hours. Before straining, agitate threads and spirit to incorporate color. Fine-strain threads out before using.

Kevin Diedrich, Pacific Cocktail Haven, San Francisco

LUST FOR LIFE
PINEAPPLE COZIES UP TO SHERRY'S NUTTY EMBRACE

Joaquín Simó created this drink for Pouring Ribbons in 2012. The stunner starts with a bang of mezcal, easing into the secondary ingredients with style. "Despite its rich flavors of spice and chocolate, Palo Cortado sherry is a very dry wine with plenty of acidity," Simó says. "The use of orgeat to sweeten the drink further echoes the nutty notes of the sherry, while the bright acidity of fresh-pressed pineapple and lemon juices keeps the drink balanced and refreshing."

1½ OUNCES Del Maguey Vida mezcal

¾ OUNCE Lustau Palo Cortado Peninsula sherry

¾ OUNCE orgeat syrup

½ OUNCE fresh lemon juice

½ OUNCE fresh pineapple juice

Combine all ingredients in a mixing tin, add ice, and shake well. Strain into a rocks glass over a large chunk of ice. Garnish with a light dusting of cocoa powder.

Joaquín Simó, Pouring Ribbons, New York City

THE AHUMADO SECO

POTENT HIBISCUS LEANS INTO SMOKE

Armed with the goal of creating an easygoing drink with a good dose of gumption, New Waterloo director of operations Nate Wales turned to dry hibiscus leaves for the foundation of the Ahumado Seco (whose name means "dry smoke"). "I love hibiscus in all forms: agua fresca, teas, sodas, et cetera," he explains. "Since the hibiscus leaf can be very tart, many add a ton of sugar for balance, but they often wind up with a sweet and syrupy mess. My intent was to brew the dried leaves as a super tart and dry [seco] tea and then find a spirit that carried its own flavor for balance. Mezcal's smokiness [ahumado] was the perfect option, so I began there. I'm overly in love with ginger, so I added that to bring some more big-gun flavor that could stand up in the mix." When all of the ingredients collide in the glass, a pleasing mellowness emerges.

> **1½ OUNCES** Mezcal Unión
>
> **¾ OUNCE** ginger liqueur
>
> **2½ OUNCES** hibiscus agua fresca
>
> **ORANGE PEEL,** for garnish
>
> **GINGER ZEST,** for garnish

Shake ingredients with ice and strain into a rocks glass filled with ice. Garnish.

For the hibiscus agua fresca, simmer 1 cup of dried hibiscus, 1 quart of water, and 2 ounces (by weight) of peeled, chopped ginger in a saucepan until reduced by ⅔. Let the mixture cool. Fine-strain ingredients into a container with a lid. Add 4 ounces simple syrup and 4 ounces lemon juice and shake to emulsify.

Nate Wales, La Condesa, Austin

THE ONLY WORD

CELERY BITTERS TRANSPORT AN ICON INTO NEW TERRITORY

San Antonio cocktail maestro Jeret Peña likes the classic Last Word cocktail so much he named his third bar after the drink. Mezcal-based riffs are a dime a dozen, but Peña's takes the cake, thanks to its smooth divide of tequila and mezcal. Celery bitters dovetail beautifully with Chartreuse's botanical nature, but if you're not a fan of the stalk's signature savoriness, simply cut the bitters and tequila and increase the mezcal pour to ¾ ounce for a more straightforward mix.

- **¾ OUNCE** blanco tequila
- **¾ OUNCE** green Chartreuse
- **¾ OUNCE** maraschino
- **¾ OUNCE** lime juice
- **¼ OUNCE** Del Maguey Chichicapa mezcal
- **3 DASHES** of Bitter Truth celery bitters

Combine ingredients in a shaker tin with ice. Shake until chilled. Strain into a cocktail glass. No garnish.

Jeret Peña, Last Word, San Antonio

MEZCAL STALK

LIKE A FRUITY STREET SNACK, IN LIQUID FORM

Named after the majestic *quiote* that springs forth from the agave plant toward the end of its life, the Mezcal Stalk boasts flavors that mirror the *piña con chilito*, a popular street snack in Mexico City made with pineapple, chile, and lime. With a savvy symmetry of sweet and citrus in the drink, don't skimp on the worm salt rim for its electric contrast of spice.

1¾ OUNCES Mezcal Enmascarado 45

½ OUNCE Cointreau

1¾ OUNCES fresh pineapple juice

¾ OUNCE fresh lemon juice

¼ OUNCE agave syrup (1:1)

LEMON WEDGES, for garnish

PINEAPPLE LEAVES, for garnish

Rim an Old Fashioned glass with worm salt and set aside. Combine ingredients in a shaker tin with ice and shake until cold. Put fresh ice into the glass and strain into a cocktail glass. Garnish with lemon wedges and pineapple leaves.

Joseph Mortera, Limantour, Mexico City

DIVISION BELL

TART, BITTER ORANGE KISSES ROASTED AGAVE

The intersection of tart lime and maraschino elevates the mezcal from base note to supporting character in this memorable number from Phil Ward. Pink Floyd's seminal album served as the namesake, as the track list accompanied Ward during the homestretch of building out the bar at Mayahuel. "One of my happy places was when, nearing completion, we would have lots and lots of wood to stain," he says. "I'd stay there all by myself after everyone else was gone and drink beer, smoke a little, and listen to Pink Floyd while I stained the beams and such."

- **1½ OUNCE** Del Maguey Vida mezcal
- **¾ OUNCE** Aperol
- **½ OUNCE** maraschino liqueur
- **¾ OUNCE** fresh lime juice
- **1 GRAPEFRUIT** twist, discard

Shake mezcal, Aperol, maraschino liqueur, and lime juice together with ice. Strain into a chilled cocktail glass. Express the oils from a grapefruit peel over the top of the drink and discard.

Phil Ward, Mayahuel, New York City

CLEVER CLUB

TANGY BERRIES, FROTHY TEXTURE

A wink to the classic Clover Club, Liz Pearce from the Drifter subbed mezcal for a new audience of cocktail lovers. A little spice, dark fruits, and smoke change the personality of the original drink, while keeping the basic structure alive. Egg whites not your thing? No sweat! The drink tastes just as good without them. It'll just lose a touch of texture.

1½ MEZCAL Amarás Cupreata

½ OUNCE ruby port

½ OUNCE dry vermouth

½ OUNCE blackberry syrup

¾ OUNCE lime juice

3 DASHES Bittermens Hellfire Habanero Shrub

EGG WHITE

BLACKBERRY, for garnish

MINT SPRIG, for garnish

Combine mezcal, port, vermouth, lime juice, egg white, and syrup in a shaker tin. Shake without ice to emulsify the egg. Add ice and shake again until the tin feels cold. Double-strain into a coupe glass. Add shrub to the top of the drink and garnish.

For the blackberry syrup, combine ½ cup blackberry preserves with ½ cup sugar and 1 cup water. Bring to a boil and then reduce to simmer. Throw 2 cardamom pods into the batch and let simmer until the sugar dissolves and the cardamom flavor is fully infused (taste as you go). Double-strain solids out of the syrup and store in the refrigerator for up to a week.

Liz Pearce, The Drifter, Chicago

AFTERSHOWER FUNK

FRESH LIKE AGUA FRESCA

Chicago corner bar Estereo specializes in delicious and straightforward drinks that showcase the personality of Latin spirits. In the case of this cooler, an infinitely quaffable merger of watermelon, lime, and mezcal screams easy drinking. Don't skimp on the chili salt; that touch of chunky spice makes a world of difference in the overall experience, like biting into a slice of fresh watermelon dusted with chili powder.

1½ OUNCES Del Maguey Vida mezcal

1½ OUNCES fresh watermelon juice

½ OUNCE fresh lime juice

½ OUNCE simple syrup (adjust to taste depending on the sweetness of the watermelon juice)

CHILI SALT, for glass rim

Rim a rocks glass with chili salt and set aside. Place 2 ice cubes in the glass and add the remaining ingredients. Give it a quick but gentle stir (as to not knock any chili salt off the rim) and top with a couple more ice cubes before serving.

For the chili salt:

3 ARBOL chilies

6–7 DRIED *guajillo* peppers

160 GRAMS Maldon sea salt

ZEST OF 2 limes

De-stem and de-seed 6 or 7 dried guajillo peppers. Toast over medium heat, enough so they are blackened in spots and fragrant, but not burned. Do the same thing with 3 arbol chilies (cooking time for arbols is less). Roughly chop all chilies and blend together in a spice grinder. You should be left with around 40 grams of ground chilies. Sea salt to chili ratio should be four to one, so 160 grams of sea salt to 40 grams ground chilies. Combine in a container and zest two limes over the top of the mixture. Cover and shake vigorously until all ingredients are thoroughly combined.

Ben Fasman and Michael Rubel, Estereo, Chicago

JAMAICÓN
POTENT ANCHO MEETS SWEET HIBISCUS

In a powerful meeting of opposites, delicate, floral hibiscus contrasts with spicy ancho chili liqueur in this drink from Sabina Sabe head bartender Alfredo Corro Enríquez. Named after a phenomenon known in Mexico as Jamaicón Syndrome, which yields feelings of homesickness or nostalgia (the "disease" itself pegged in honor of 1950s soccer player José "Jamaicón" Villegas, who became so despondent for the flavors of his country while traveling for the World Cup that the nickname stuck), the drink brings flavors of Enríquez's childhood to the glass with style.

1 OUNCE Rey Campero Espadín

1 OUNCE Ancho Reyes ancho chili liqueur

1½ OUNCES spice-infused hibiscus syrup

¾ OUNCE fresh lime juice

ORANGE TWIST, for garnish

Shake ingredients together in a shaker tin with ice. Double-strain in a coupe glass, and garnish with orange twist.

For the spice-infused hibiscus syrup:

200 GRAMS dried hibiscus flowers

4 ANCHO chilies, seeded and stemmed

4 STAR anise pods

5 CINNAMON sticks

3 CUPS sugar

4 CUPS water

Toast anchos in a saucepan over medium heat until fragrant. Do not burn. Set aside. Combine hibiscus and water in a saucepan and bring to a simmer. Add toasted chili peppers and spices and raise heat to a boil. Let ingredients simmer 5–10 minutes to taste, and then remove from heat. Add 3 cups sugar and stir until dissolved. Strain spices and chilies out of the mixture into a container with a lid. Store in the fridge when not using.

Alfredo Corro Enríquez, Sabina Sabe, Oaxaca City

ELECTRON
A TRIPLE HIT OF EARTHY FLAVORS

"Bright orange, tart, smoky, spiced—the Electron has so many flavors dancing around, it felt right to give it an energetic name," says GreenRiver former head bartender Julia Momose of this vibrant cocktail. "It reminds me of what we learned about electrons in school, and I still have this image in my mind of these subatomic particles zipping around the nucleus with an unfathomable amount of energy." The zippy, kinetic vibes are just one of the many reasons why I love this carrot-spiked drink from one of Chicago's best and brightest. The fruity notes of the Don Amado wholly complement the earthy carrot juice, and the lime juice adds a zing of brightness to the combo. "Imagine roasted carrots, with just a hint of char, seasoned with cardamom and topped with a dollop of yogurt and a squeeze of lime," Momose says of the way the flavors intertwine.

1¾ OUNCES Don Amado Rústico mezcal

½ OUNCE cinnamon syrup

¾ OUNCE fresh lime juice

¾ OUNCE fresh carrot juice

2 DASHES Regan's Orange Bitters

PINK PEPPERCORN, for rim

SALT, for rim

Combine ingredients in a shaker tin with ice. Shake until the tin feels cold. Strain into a coupe glass. Garnish.

For cinnamon syrup, combine 1½ cups water with 1¼ cups sugar, and 3 tablespoons cinnamon bark (or cracked sticks). Bring to a boil and let simmer for 20 minutes. Remove from heat and strain off the cinnamon bark. Label and keep refrigerated until ready to use.

Julia Momose, GreenRiver, Chicago

SORRY FOR HARAMBE
REMINISCENT OF FALL, IN ALL THE RIGHT WAYS

A liquid ode to one unlucky gorilla, the Sorry for Harambe is a prime example of Jay Schroeder's dialed-in flavor combinations and penchant for pop-culture references during his time mixing at Mezcaleria Las Flores in Chicago. Flavor-wise, the cocktail screams autumn, with honeyed figs and fragrant guajillo peppers layering gently over a malty bedrock of genever. The mezcal anchors the medley, and a scant touch of absinthe bridges the gap between the high notes of citrus and the rest of the seasonal flavors.

- **1½ OUNCES** Mayalen Machetazo Cupreata Mezcal
- **¾ OUNCE** fresh lemon juice
- **¾ OUNCE** guajillo-fig syrup
- **½ OUNCE** Bols Genever
- **½ BAR SPOON** absinthe
- **CRUSHED PECANS,** for glass rim

Combine all ingredients in a shaker tin and shake over ice. Strain into a clay bowl half-rimmed with crushed pecans and serve.

To make the guajillo-fig syrup, de-stem and toast 6 dried guajillo chilies. Collect 180 grams of dried mission figs. Add both ingredients to 1 quart of water and blend until smooth. Add to saucepan with 1 quart water and simmer for 10 minutes. Strain through a chinois before bottling.

Jay Schroeder, Mezcaleria Las Flores, Chicago

MANZAÑILLA SYLVESTRE

A GRACEFUL, LEMON-TINTED REFRESHER

Built on a base of soothing chamomile tea (*manzañilla* is the Spanish word for chamomile), this sunshine-fueled sipper advertises equal parts substance and perk. For the recipe, Mezcalito beverage director Guadalupe Jaques took loose inspiration from the Corpse Reviver No. 2. To make his mark, Jaques ditched the gin, liqueur, and absinthe, and introduced mezcal and a warming tea syrup to the scheme. The results: beautiful lemon notes layered over a bed of grassy agave and floral chamomile.

> **1 OUNCE** Mezcal Unión
>
> **1 OUNCE** Lillet Blanc
>
> **1 OUNCE** fresh lemon juice
>
> **1 OUNCE** citrus-chamomile tea syrup
>
> **LEMON TWIST,** for garnish

Add all ingredients to a shaker tin. Shake vigorously and double-strain into a coupe glass. Garnish with a lemon twist.

For the citrus-chamomile tea syrup, combine 1 cup sugar and 1 cup hot water in a saucepan and bring to a boil. Reduce quickly and let simmer until the sugar has dissolved. Remove from heat and add 1–2 tea bags (to taste). Allow to steep at room temperature for 24 hours. Remove tea bags and store syrup in the fridge when not in use.

Guadalupe Jaques, Mezcalito, San Francisco

TIP: **A quick Google search will reveal that citrus-chamomile tea can be purchased online. Jaques uses Lamill brand.**

APIUM (OPIUM)

CELERY STEALS THE SHOW IN THIS PRETTY DAISY

The vibes at Mexico City cocktail bar Baltra are pretty damn sexy. In the tiny but cozy space, the barkeeps exude a cool confidence and the cocktail menu (inspired by Darwin's travels to the Galapagos Islands) is an impressive representation of their natural talent. At a glance, the popular Apium, also known as the Opium, ticks off all the boxes of the classic margarita, but don't be fooled—with the addition of celery bitters, a savory magic comes into play and the combo is transformed into something far more craveable. Ridiculously easy to make, it's a refreshing go-to when you're in the mood for something simple yet satisfying.

> **1½ OUNCES** espadín
>
> **1 OUNCE** fresh lime juice
>
> **¾ OUNCE** simple syrup
>
> **4 DASHES** celery bitters
>
> **CELERY SALT,** for garnish

Combine ingredients in a shaker tin and shake with ice. Strain into the prepared rocks glass over fresh ice. Sprinkle celery salt over the top of the drink to garnish.

Daniel Reyes, Baltra, Mexico City

PUA LANI
A BEAUTIFULLY BALANCED TROPICAL TIPPLE

Misfit characters collide in this nouveau tiki mix from Del Maguey "Madrina" Misty Kalkofen. Instead of fighting for the spotlight, each component merges seamlessly, with the black currant–like sloe gin and clove-heavy falernum sweetening the citrus and bitter coffee liqueur elements. Mezcal has yet to solidify a recurring role within the canon of tiki drinks, but if this recipe is any indication, the nuanced depths of the spirit have great potential in the genre.

2 OUNCES Del Maguey Vida mezcal

¾ OUNCE sloe gin

¼ OUNCE coffee liqueur

½ OUNCE velvet falernum

¾ OUNCE pineapple juice

½ OUNCE fresh lemon juice

Dry-shake all ingredients to incorporate. Strain into your favorite tiki mug filled with crushed ice. Garnish with a healthy sprig of mint.

Misty Kalkofen, Del Maguey Single Village Mezcal

SINGLE VILLAGE FIX
VISCOUS PINEAPPLE SYRUP MEETS A MINERAL BASELINE

Thad Vogler has always been interested in spirits with clear agricultural origins, so it's no surprise he chose the bold punch of Del Maguey's Single Village (hence the title) Chichicapa for this cocktail. "According to some old [recipe books], a fix was anything sweetened with pineapple," he explains. "Most of the books we use were written before agave spirits had become widely used in the US, but the interaction of the piña from the maguey and a real piña seemed like an obvious one." The drink was created during Vogler's time at Beretta, but he later adjusted the measurements to suit the menu at San Francisco's Bar Agricole, where the drink quickly became a modern classic within the contemporary cocktail movement.

> 1½ **OUNCES** Del Maguey Chichicapa mezcal
>
> ½ **OUNCE** fresh lime juice
>
> ½ **OUNCE** pineapple gum syrup

Combine the ingredients with ice in a shaker, and shake. Strain into a chilled cocktail glass and serve. No garnish. For best results, seek out commercial pineapple gum syrup, such as the one from Small Hand Foods or Liber & Co.

Thad Vogler, Bar Agricole, San Francisco

BOOZY

STIRRED NUMBERS FOR THE ADVENTUROUS DRINKER

MEZCAL NEGRONI

AN ICONIC TRIFECTA, WITH A TWIST

The Negroni tastes great with almost any kind of base spirit, and mezcal is no exception. Andrew Abrahamson, director of operations for 213 Hospitality Single Spirit Bars, says the Las Perlas staff chose mezcal instead of tequila for the house Negroni because of the spirit's broader mouthfeel and more complex flavors. "I don't want to sell tequila short, but it's typically a little one-dimensional and can be beat up by vermouth and Campari," he explains. "Almost any mezcal you can find will work well." For the sweet vermouth, the barkeeps offer options—Dolin for a lighter texture, or Carpano Antica for a more robust flavor and fuller body.

1 OUNCE Del Maguey Vida mezcal

¾ OUNCE sweet vermouth

¾ OUNCE Campari

ORANGE TWIST, for garnish

Combine ingredients in a mixing glass with ice. Stir until chilled. Serve either up in a coupe or on the rocks in an Old Fashioned glass. Garnish.

Andrew Abrahamson, Las Perlas, Los Angeles

OAXACA OLD FASHIONED
THE KING OF MEZCAL COCKTAILS

Widely known as the quintessential calling card of mezcal cocktails, the Oaxaca Old Fashioned was developed by bartender Phil Ward during his time at Death & Co., but the uncomplicated yet memorable union of tequila, mezcal, agave nectar, and bitters rose to fame on the menu at Mayahuel. Now it's widely heralded as the drink that communicated the potential and versatility of the spirit in the cocktail world. The recipe hasn't aged a day. One sip, and you'll be hooked.

1½ OUNCES El Tesoro reposado tequila

½ OUNCE Del Maguey San Luis del Rio mezcal

1 BAR spoon agave nectar

2 DASHES Angostura bitters

FLAMED ORANGE TWIST, for garnish

Mix the tequila, mezcal, agave nectar, and bitters in a mixing glass with ice. Strain over a fresh rock in an Old Fashioned glass. Flame an orange peel over the top of the drink, and rest the twist in the glass as a garnish.

Phil Ward, Mayahuel, New York City

THE BRAVE

AN INTENSE HIT OF CARAMELIZED ORANGE AND SMOKE

With a bold composition and even more daring execution, this heavyweight isn't for the faint of heart. Created by Houston barman Bobby Heugel, the Brave landed on the opening menu at Anvil Bar & Refuge in 2009. As unique as it is recognizable—its recipe is considered an icon in the cocktail world, referenced in books, magazines, and blogs galore—the drink is served in an uncommon manner. Instead of the typical shake or stir, the Brave greets the guest at room temperature, after a quick swirl of the bar spoon in the glass to incorporate the ingredients. Expect flavors of roasted orange, nutmeg, clove, and smoke coming together with finesse and attitude.

1 OUNCE Del Maguey Vida mezcal

1 OUNCE Siembra Azul blanco tequila

½ OUNCE Averna

¼ OUNCE Royal Combier

ANGOSTURA BITTERS

ORANGE PEEL, for garnish

Combine mezcal, tequila, Averna, and Combier in a wine glass and stir to incorporate. Do not chill; instead serve at room temperature. To garnish, using a mister filled with Angostura bitters, spray three quick mists over the top of the drink. If you don't have a mister, a few small drops will do the trick.

Bobby Heugel, Anvil Bar & Refuge, Houston

WHITE OLD FASHIONED

A HAUNTING LOVE LETTER TO MEZCAL AND CHOCOLATE

When it comes to Old Fashioned–style cocktails (spirit, sweetener, bitters), most folks go the aged spirits route, taking notes from bourbon's legacy. Yet Melrose Umbrella Company program director Dave Purcell found success when uniting mezcal and cacao instead. "I was chasing the roasted, slightly smoky effect of mezcal and honeyed liqueurs, which was pretty basic. But then I had the idea of smoke and chocolate, which became the obsessive flavor," he says. "I tried it as a sour, as a Manhattan, as a shot. It ultimately came down to the crème de cacao, and it had to be Old Fashioned style." The salient smoke and chocolate flavors shine through, mingling harmoniously with yellow Chartreuse.

> **2 OUNCES** Mezcal El Silencio
>
> **½ OUNCE** (scant) Marie Brizard White Crème de Cacao
>
> **BAR SPOON** Yellow Chartreuse
>
> **1 DASH** Regan's Orange Bitters
>
> **LEMON PEEL,** for garnish

Stir ingredients together in a mixing glass and strain over 1 large ice cube. Garnish with an expressed lemon peel.

Dave Purcell, Melrose Umbrella Company, Los Angeles

LIP SPIN #2

A CURL-UP-BY-THE-FIREPLACE KIND OF NIGHTCAP (LEFT)

For the love of all things dark, earthy, and bitter! This gorgeous gem is a deep cut from the Strange Stirrings section of Mayahuel's cocktail menu. Striking a beautiful tension between velvety dried fruits and crunchy bitterness, it's all tobacco and leather, laced with wrinkled fig, overripe cherry, and dry artichoke.

1½ OUNCES mezcal cupreata

¾ OUNCE sloe gin

¾ OUNCE Cynar

Served up. No garnish.

Phil Ward, Mayahuel, New York City

ONLY TO CONSIDER

A VERSATILE AMALGAMATION OF BOOZY, BITTER, AND SWEET

My mother is an unabashed Rick Bayless fan, and the first time she tasted this number from his new mezcal-focused bar and restaurant, her eyes lit up. I knew we had a hit on our hands before she even passed the glass my way. With simultaneously edgy and elegant qualities, this bullet of a drink easily serves as either apéritif or digestif, given one's mood. Leña Brava spirits director Jeff Walters assembled the keen balance of sweet crema de mezcal (mezcal plus agave nectar) and bittersweet Campari and Fernet. The dry curacao ties the loose ends together with a lovely caramelized orange note.

1½ OUNCES Del Maguey Crema de Mezcal

¾ OUNCE Pierre Ferrand Dry Curaçao

½ OUNCE Campari

¼ OUNCE Letherbee Fernet

1 DASH Angostura bitters

ORANGE PEEL, for garnish

Stir all ingredients in a mixing glass with ice until chilled. Strain into a Nick and Nora glass or small coupe. Express a fresh orange peel over the top of the cocktail then discard.

Jeff Walters, Leña Brava, Chicago

EL VAMPIRO

LUSH, CRIMSON-HUED ELEGANCE

A mineral-driven espadín from the state of Guerrero lays the groundwork for sweet cassis and nutty sherry in this sumptuous creation from San Francisco. To bring a pleasing acidity to the potion, Forgery partner Jacques Bezuidenhout reaches for acid phosphate instead of citrus. "Using lemon juice really muddied up the color of the cocktail and dominated some of the delicate flavors, so the acid phosphate was a perfect addition. It added the desired acid to balance out the cocktail and it retained its clarity in the glass." Consider it a sultry, south-of-the-border answer to the Italian apéritif.

> **1½ OUNCES** Mezcal Amarás Espadín
>
> **¾ OUNCE** manzanilla sherry
>
> **½ OUNCE** Giffard crème de cassis
>
> **2 DASHES** acid phosphate
>
> **2 DROPS** saltwater
>
> **LEMON TWIST,** for garnish

Build ingredients in a mixing glass and fill with ice. Stir and strain in a Nick and Nora glass. Garnish with a small lemon twist.

Jacques Bezuidenhout, Forgery, San Francisco

TIP: Acid phosphate sounds intimidating, but it's quite easy to find, and even easier to use. Simply substitute a few dashes in a recipe instead of citrus juice to achieve a similar balance between acid, booze, and sugar.

MAYOR ROCK

AN AUTUMNAL, RUSTIC BLEND WITH HIGH CITRUS NOTES

Apples are often used to fortify pechuga, as the warm, fruity notes bring extra character to the bones of a good mezcal. Ricky Gomez created this stirred cocktail for a favorite regular at Teardrop Lounge in Portland, Oregon. The drink didn't appear on a menu until he worked behind the stick at (now shuttered) Riffle. Gomez reaches for Del Maguey Santo Domingo Albarradas for the recipe—an espadín with a honeyed roast agave infrastructure and bright guava, grapefruit, and pineapple overtones that brighten the baking spice bouquet of high-proof apple brandy.

- **1 OUNCE** Del Maguey Santo Domingo Albarradas mezcal
- **1 OUNCE** bonded apple brandy
- **1 TEASPOON** agave nectar
- **2 DASHES** Angostura bitters
- **1 DASH** orange bitters

Build ingredients together in a rocks glass. Add ice and stir until chilled. Garnish with an orange peel.

Ricky Gomez, Riffle, Portland, OR

AGE OF DISCOVERY
MOLASSES DOMINATES THIS STIRRED JEWEL

Former Pastry War general manager Kehlen Selph found her muse for this recipe via a drink called the Cucaracha Rum, a blackstrap-heavy cocktail from a 1920s bar in Mexico City called La Cucaracha Cocktail Club. "There was no mezcal on the menu, but this was a classic cocktail from Mexico City in the 1920s, so I wanted to use it as inspiration and see what it would taste like with mezcal," Selph says. The results of her modern sorcery are impressive. Heaps of dark, molasses-like sugars and notes of overripe pear counterbalance subtle hints of orange blossom, with mezcal acting as a vigorous undercurrent of smoke.

¾ OUNCE Cruzan Blackstrap rum

¾ OUNCE Del Maguey Vida mezcal

½ OUNCE Luxardo maraschino liqueur

¼ OUNCE turbinado and raw maguey sap syrup (a 1:1 ratio)

1 DASH Angostura bitters

NANCHE BERRIES, for garnish (substitute maraschino cherry)

Stir ingredients together with ice in a rocks glass. Garnish with nanches.

For the turbinado and raw maguey sap syrup, bring one part turbinado sugar and one part water to a boil in a saucepan. Boil until sugar dissolves and set aside. In another saucepan, bring one part maguey sap and one part water to a boil and cook until sugars dissolve. Combine both syrups together in a container with a lid. Keep refrigerated until use.

Maguey sap can be bought from several online retailers and in Mexican markets in certain states. The thick, molasses-like syrup is like normal agave syrup turned up to eleven; its dense, concentrated flavor is not unlike tasting raw roasted agave straight from the oven. It's not really an ingredient that can be substituted.

Kehlen Selph, the Pastry War, Houston

> TIP: Nanche is a small, bright yellow berry. Grown mostly in South America and Mexico, you can sometimes find them at Mexican markets. If not, a maraschino cherry will get the job done just fine.

OAKLAND

SOPHISTICATED, WITH DEEP CHOCOLATE NOTES AND A SLIGHT KICK OF COFFEE

Cupreata sets a floral tone in this boozy blend from former Trick Dog manager Caitlin Laman. The mezcal boosts rhubarb-based Cappelletti Sfumato Amaro (which adds its own thin veil of smoke), and a little bit of chicory spice sneaks into the recipe by way of St. George NOLA Coffee Liqueur's. Together, the drink resolves in a smart harmony of bittersweet coffee, smoke, and dried-fruit flavors.

1½ OUNCES Mezcal Amarás Cupreata

½ OUNCE Cappelletti Sfumato Amaro

¼ OUNCE St. George NOLA Coffee Liqueur

¼ OUNCE simple syrup

2 DASHES Angostura bitters

ORANGE TWIST, for garnish

LEMON TWIST, for garnish

Stir ingredients together in a mixing glass with ice until chilled. Strain into an Old Fashioned glass on the rocks. Garnish.

Caitlin Laman, Dirty Precious, Brooklyn

MIDNIGHT MARAUDER

THE DARK AND TWISTY SIBLING OF THE NEGRONI

There are about a million ways you can tweak the framework of the classic Negroni (gin, Campari, and sweet vermouth), but this unorthodox imagining from New York barman Joaquín Simó does a primo job of evoking the indigenous flavors of Oaxaca. Mole bitters and the softly bitter Bonal combine for a dark, chocolatey backbone, and when artichoke-heavy Cynar enters the equation, those notes are amplified. If Oaxaca's delectable red mole transformed into a dignified drink, this would be it.

1 OUNCE Del Maguey Vida mezcal

1 OUNCE Bonal Gentiane Quina

1 OUNCE Cynar

1 DASH Bittermens mole bitters

Combine all ingredients in a mixing glass, add ice, and stir briskly. Strain into a chilled Nick and Nora glass. No garnish.

Joaquín Simó, Pouring Ribbons, New York City

TIP: **Smith & Cross brings unmatchable depth to the drink, but if you don't have any on hand, reach for another Jamaican rum for similar results.**

BETTER & BETTER

BAKED BANANA AND VANILLA MEET VEGETAL AGAVE

Bartender Jan Warren's admiration for mezcal was sparked during his first trip to Oaxaca. "I bought my first bottle from a man with no shoes and a canvas bag full of repurposed coke bottles containing a funky-smelling, clear liquid. I drank it on a beach, lying in the sun. I was hooked." In his borderline tropical twist on the classic Old Fashioned, Fidencio's Clásico espadín serves as anchor, bolstered by the sweet spice of falernum and the *hogo* funk of Jamaican rum. Warren presented the drink to Fidencio partner Arik Torren at the bar one night to get his feedback. Torren found the first sip a touch abrasive, but exclaimed, "This drink gets better and better" as the ice slowly melted. "I don't remember if it was him or me that really named the drink, but he said it first, and it just made perfect sense," Warren says.

> 1½ **OUNCES** Fidencio Clásico mezcal
>
> ½ **OUNCE** Smith & Cross Jamaican rum
>
> ¼ **OUNCE** velvet falernum
>
> **LEMON TWIST,** for garnish

Combine falernum, rum, and mezcal in a rocks glass. Add ice and stir until chilled. Garnish with lemon twist.

Jan Warren, Dutch Kills, Long Island City, NY

INTREPID

A HYPER-SAVORY, STIRRED DELIGHT

Named after the historic aircraft carrier USS *Intrepid* docked in the Hudson River, Eryn Reece's audacious take on the Manhattan is a brooding beauty. Spicy rye whiskey makes up most of the design, but mezcal sneaks in to contribute an underlying current of caramelized agave. Cynar brings an almost stalwart dryness to the glass. Boasting a perfect synthesis of bitter and sweet, it's a memorable drink worthy of legendary nightcap status.

> **1½ OUNCES** rye whiskey
>
> **½ OUNCE** Del Maguey Vida mezcal
>
> **¾ OUNCE** Cynar
>
> **¾ OUNCE** Carpano Bianco vermouth
>
> **1 DASH** celery bitters

Combine ingredients in a mixing glass with ice. Stir until chilled. Strain into a Nick and Nora glass. No garnish.

Eryn Reece, Sons & Daughters, New York City

POLAR BEAR

MINTY FRESH, WITH AN ARCTIC ATTITUDE

Echoing elements of the classic Stinger cocktail—traditionally a split of brandy and crème de menthe—the frosty Polar Bear first made a splash on the inaugural menu at Trick Dog when it opened in early 2013. Without the vanilla and oak notes from the brandy, the cooling personality of crème de menthe packs twice the potency, and the mezcal's inherent minerality helps keep the sipper crisp and balanced.

1½ OUNCES Montelobos mezcal

¾ OUNCE blanc vermouth

½ OUNCE crème de menthe

6 DROPS celery bitters

Combine ingredients in a mixing tin. Add ice and shake until chilled. Strain into a Nick and Nora glass. No garnish.

The Bon Vivants, Trick Dog, San Francisco

TIP: **Common bartending sense would normally dictate a quick stir with ice to dilute (because there's no citrus juice in the recipe), but resist the urge and give this one a good shake to whip the crème de menthe with the other ingredients. A foggy louche will emerge, giving the final product an alluring, mystical quality that's as pleasing to look at as it is to sip.**

FIZZY

SODA, BEER, AND SPARKLING WINE MAKE FOR SNAPPY HIGHBALLS

PAPA DIABLO
DRAMATIC IN BOTH APPEARANCE AND FLAVOR

For his version of the El Diablo cocktail, Barrio spirits director Casey Robison drops the tequila in favor of Nuestra Soledad's robust espadín. It's a powerful remix of the flavorful highball, with mezcal lending a noticeable swagger to the mix of cassis, ginger beer, and lime juice. A quick pressing of fresh ginger in the tin helps amplify the root's trademark spice.

- **3 THIN SLICES** fresh ginger
- **2 OUNCES** Nuestra Soledad Espadín
- **½ OUNCE** fresh lime juice
- **¼ OUNCE** crème de cassis
- **¼ OUNCE** agave syrup
- **2 DASHES** Angostura bitters
- **GINGER BEER**
- **THIN SLICE** ginger, for garnish
- **LIME WHEEL,** for garnish

In a shaker, tamp down 3 thin slices of ginger to express the flavors. Add ice and shake until chilled. Strain into a Collins glass. Add crushed ice, and top with ginger beer. Garnish with a thin slice of ginger and a lime wheel

Casey Robison, Barrio, Seattle

RAICILLA BATANGA

A SURPRISINGLY AGREEABLE COMBO OF SEEMINGLY DISPARATE INGREDIENTS

It might seem counterintuitive to bring together something as beautiful and expressive as raicilla with something so rudimentary as cola. Yet, that's the beauty of Palenque Mezcaleria's version of the classic Batanga. Normally made with tequila and coke, in this case, floor manager Nathan Schmit prefers the complexity of mezcal. "When mixed with coke, raicilla becomes a 'full' experience for the mouth, mixing sweetness with the already present floral, citrus, and vegetal characteristics," he says. "It is like hearing a beautiful violin solo, and then hearing that violin play with an entire orchestra."

1½ OUNCES La Venenosa Raicilla Sierra Occidental

HALF LIME

SALT

MEXICAN COCA-COLA

Fill a Collins glass with fresh cubed ice. Sprinkle a touch of salt on the ice. Add raicilla, squeeze the lime into the glass, and stir to incorporate ingredients. Top with Coca-Cola.

Nathan Schmit, Palenque Mezcaleria, Denver

DIZZY OAXACAN

A SPLENDID, BUBBLY CROWD-PLEASER

In 2011, I decided it would be a great idea to spread the gospel of mezcal with a festive holiday punch. After finding the Dizzy Oaxacan by cocktail consultant Tad Carducci, I got to work on the details but developed a few reservations as the date neared. Picturing my beer-drinking uncles and wine-loving aunts getting their first hit of mezcal, I worried I might have made a grave mistake by bringing this exotic brew to the table. Alas, I stood corrected. Everyone lapped it up, and praised the recipe with each helping. Moral of the story: The synthesis of ginger beer and mezcal never fails, and when bolstered with the winter spices of Italian amaro, it's a smash hit primed for even the pickiest of drinkers.

> **1½ OUNCES** Del Maguey Vida mezcal
>
> **¾ OUNCE** Amaro Lucano
>
> **½ OUNCE** fresh grapefruit juice
>
> **½ OUNCE** fresh lemon juice
>
> **2–3 OUNCES** ginger beer
>
> **GRAPEFRUIT WEDGE** dusted with cayenne, for garnish

Combine mezcal, Lucano, grapefruit juice, lemon juice, and simple syrup together in a shaker tin. Add ice and shake. Strain into a Collins glass filled with ice. Top off with ginger beer and garnish. To scale up for a punch, check out the specs listed in Carducci's 2015 cocktail book, *The Tippling Bros. A Lime and a Shaker: Discovering Mexican-Inspired Cocktails*.

Tad Carducci, cofounder of the Tippling Bros., New York City

LETTERS FROM OAXACA

A CLASSY APÉRITIF WITH HONEY NOTES

Mezcal and rosé make for a surprisingly melodic match, and in this effervescent sparkler from Portland bartender Alex von Holdt, honey and lime tie up the loose ends. It's a great introduction to the spirit, but von Holdt warns the drink packs a startling amount of booze, so approach with caution. "Clean, simple, and deceptively inebriating, I personally saw this particular parcel leave many unsuspecting patrons askew by night's end," he says, "and before long I began imploring the general public to partake in these for longer than thirty seconds at a time . . ."

1 OUNCE dry sparkling rosé (cava)

1½ OUNCES Del Maguey Vida mezcal

¾ OUNCE fresh lime

¾ OUNCE honey syrup

1 DASH Peychaud's bitters, for garnish

Prepare a coupe glass by pouring the sparkling wine in first and set aside. Combine the mezcal, lime, and honey syrup in a shaker tin with ice and shake until chilled. Strain into the coupe glass so the ingredients fully combine. Add one dash Peychaud's bitters to finish.

For the honey syrup, combine 1 cup honey and 1 cup water in a saucepan. Bring to a boil and reduce heat to simmer. Let simmer until the consistency looks even and remove from heat.

Alex von Holdt, High Noon, Portland

BLIND LEMON JEFFERSON
MEZCAL SINGS WITH BITTERSWEET APEROL

Will Elliott pegs this frothy creation as a "desert-oriented, psychedelic fizz with south-of-the-border leanings." Originally called the Moonshake, Elliott adapted the recipe for the menu at Maison Premiere in Brooklyn and updated the title to Blind Lemon Jefferson, a nod to the popular early-twentieth-century blues singer and guitarist. It left the bar's menu years ago, but continues to be ordered by regular guests, proving its staying power.

- **1½ OUNCES** Del Maguey Vida mezcal
- **1 OUNCE** Aperol
- **½ OUNCE** fresh grapefruit juice
- **½ OUNCE** fresh lemon juice
- **¾ OUNCE** simple syrup
- **¾ OUNCE** egg white (or the white from one egg)
- **4 HARD** dashes grapefruit bitters
- **CLUB SODA**
- **1–2 SMALL** mint sprigs, for garnish

Combine ingredients in a shaker tin with ice. Shake until chilled. Strain into a Collins glass without ice. Top with club soda. Garnish with a mint sprig.

Will Elliott, Maison Premiere, Brooklyn

MEZCAL GINGER PALOMA

A PEPPERY ALTERNATIVE TO TRADITION

Bending the specs of the Paloma ever so slightly, this spicy update from Half Step bar owner Chris Bostick is primed to cut the edge off any sweltering Texas afternoon. Mezcal contributes an unmatchable depth to the Paloma, and when a tiny bit of ginger syrup comes into play a complexity emerges that's tough to beat. Look for the freshest grapefruits to complement, and adjust the soda to taste.

> **2 OUNCES** Del Maguey Vida mezcal
>
> **½ OUNCE** fresh ruby red grapefruit juice
>
> **½ OUNCE** fresh lime juice
>
> **¼ OUNCE** ginger syrup
>
> **2½ OUNCES** Jarritos grapefruit soda

Shake all ingredients except for soda with 2 tablespoons crushed ice. Pour into an ice-filled Collins glass, top with soda, and garnish with grapefruit wedge and a pinch of kosher salt.

Chris Bostick, Half Step, Austin

¡FÉNIX! MICHELADA

AN EXPLOSION OF VERDANT GOODNESS, FIZZED OUT WITH MEXICAN LAGER

When I asked the Bon Vivants for their favorite mezcal Michelada recipe, I (somewhat foolishly) expected your standard tomato-based specs, maybe with some unusual spices. Imagine my delight when they sent this outside-the-box invention. Brimming with savory flavor and a spike of heat from the poblano-based Ancho Verde, it's a smart representation of how a Michelada made with mezcal should taste: effervescent, with flavors that frame and support the vegetal nature of the spirit instead of masking its soul, as tomato juice is apt to do.

- **1½ OUNCES** Montelobos Mezcal
- **1 OUNCE** celery juice
- **½ OUNCE** Ancho Verde chili liqueur
- **½ OUNCE** simple syrup
- **½ OUNCE** lime juice

Rim half a highball glass with salt and set aside. Combine mezcal, celery juice, Ancho Verde, syrup, and lime in a shaker tin with ice. Shake until chilled and strain into a highball glass with ice. Top with an ice-cold Mexican lager.

The Bon Vivants, Trick Dog, San Francisco

MEZCAL MULE

A CLASSIC RECIPE GONE ROGUE

Long the territory of vodka drinkers, the drinking landscape of West Hollywood has started to shift as of late, thanks to the help of mezcal pioneers like the team at Gracias Madre. Beverage director Jason Eisner creates new agave lovers daily with an approachable menu full of mezcal- and tequila-based cocktails. For beginners, he recommends the Mezcal Mule. "The Mule is perfect for someone who wants to have a comfortable experience—for people who have had Moscow Mules before but are looking for a bit more complexity." For added freshness, Eisner adds cold-pressed lime and ginger juice, but for home bartenders, he recommends buying a good-quality ginger beer, like Q or Fever Tree. "If the soda you're using is too sweet, up the percentage of citrus a bit to balance it out," he says.

- **2 OUNCES** Mezcal Vago Espadín
- **½ OUNCE** fresh lime juice
- **½ OUNCE** ginger juice
- **1 OUNCE** agave nectar
- **1½ OUNCES** sparkling water

Add all ingredients to a cocktail shaker and dry shake. Careful—the bubbles in the soda water will give a little pushback, but don't sweat it! Strain into a copper mule mug and add fresh rocks. Garnish with a sprig of mint and a quartered lime (optional).

Jason Eisner, Gracias Madre, Los Angeles

GINGER CUCUMBER HIGHBALL
ESSENTIAL SPRINGTIME SIPPING

Perfectly aligned with the no-frills sensibility of Mexico's popular *refrescos*, this warm-weather highball is almost too easy to crush. The recipe—a refreshing blend of cucumber, ginger, and lime juice—was a collaborative effort from the crew at Espita in Washington, D.C., when the bar first opened in 2016 and has been a crowd favorite ever since. El Buho brings a nice, soft base note to the sprightly flavors, acting as a gentle reminder that mezcal works well with almost any kind of fresh juice.

1½ OUNCES El Buho mezcal

¾ OUNCE lime juice

¾ OUNCE ginger-cucumber syrup

4 OUNCES soda water

LONG, THIN cucumber slice, for garnish

Add ice to a highball glass, then pour in each of the ingredients. Give the drink a light stir with a straw. Roll the cucumber slice and use it as a garnish.

For ginger-cucumber syrup, in a tightly sealed jar shake together 5 ounces cucumber juice, 1 ounce ginger juice, and 5 ounces sugar until the sugar is dissolved. To juice the ginger and cucumber, use a juicer or a blender. If using the latter, add a little water to the ginger before blending. Strain each juice through a fine-mesh sieve.

Espita, Washington, D.C.

FESTIVE

PUNCH, BRUNCH, AND MORE

VAGO CHAMPURRADO
HOT CHOCOLATE, OAXACAN-STYLE

In the States, you don't see champurrado—a piping-hot masa-based drink flavored with chocolate—on menus very often, but with its thicker consistency and roots in Mexican culture, it's one of the best hot chocolates to spike with mezcal. Jessica Sanders of drink.well and Backbeat in Austin picked up her recipe from her great-aunts and grandmother, who would whip up batches with masa flour left over from making tamales on New Year's Eve. Sanders has since added mezcal and debuted her adult version at both bars.

For the booze, she uses Mezcal Vago Elote for its corn-infused goodness that mirrors the masa in the drink. "Elote is, in my opinion, one of the most approachable entry-level mezcals because it is earthy and sweet on the palate with an herbaceous little kick of peppermint on the finish," she says. "That creamy mouthfeel was such a great complement to a sweet, rich, thick beverage like the champurrado—and the minty back note is a lovely little surprise on the end that really comes out with the chocolate."

1½ OUNCES Mezcal Vago Elote

5 OUNCES hot champurrado

Pour hot champurrado into a mug and add mezcal. Stir to incorporate. Optional: Grate fresh cinnamon over the top or add a pinch of smoked sea salt for an extra savory kick. For the champurrado:

½ CUP (by volume) corn masa flour

6 OUNCES (by weight) Mexican chocolate (Abuelita discs are ideal)

3 CUPS whole milk (must be whole milk—skim or 2 percent cannot be substituted here!)

1½ CUPS boiling water

3 TABLESPOONS packed piloncillo (Mexican brown sugar)

⅛ TEASPOON kosher salt

Dissolve the flour into the boiling water, stirring until few to no clumps appear. In a saucepan over medium heat, warm the whole milk, stirring frequently to avoid burning. When hot, add the chocolate and piloncillo sugar and cook until all the chocolate and sugar has completely dissolved. (Note: Cutting the chocolate into smaller chunks expedites this process.) Once the chocolate has dissolved, slowly add the hot masa flour water, stirring regularly. Continue to simmer and stir until the beverage is thick. Add the salt at the very end and stir. Yields approximately 1 liter (or 6 individual servings), and can be kept hot in an air pot for 4–6 hours.

Jessica Sanders, drink.well and Backbeat, Austin

ESPUMITA BLANCA

FOR FANS OF THE WHITE RUSSIAN

From the beverage carts of Mexico City to the lunch tables of mezcal-producing families all over Oaxaca, creamy horchata is one of the most recognizable drinks of Mexico. NIDO co-owner Cory McCollow aimed to nudge the humble beverage to the next level by adding "a little kick" via equal parts sweet Del Maguey Crema de Mezcal and Siembra Valles reposado tequila. When layered with a boozy ounce of chicory-spiced New Orleans–style coffee liqueur, the Espumita Blanca—or white foam, named for the way the ice cube ends up "hidden" in the glass—makes for a fun mesh of cultural flavors. I'd keep things simple and use a store-bought horchata for the drink, but if you want to mix to NIDO's specifications, the recipe is included below.

¾ OUNCE Del Maguey Crema de Mezcal

1 OUNCE St. George NOLA coffee liqueur

¾ OUNCE Siembra Valles reposado tequila

2 OUNCES horchata

GRATED NUTMEG, for garnish

Combine all ingredients in a shaker. Fill with ice and shake. Double-strain over a big ice cube in a rocks glass. Garnish with grated nutmeg.

For the horchata:

½ CUP organic white rice

2 GRAMS Mexican cinnamon stick (not ground)

½ CUP granulated sugar

WHOLE ORGANIC milk

1 TEASPOON vanilla extract

Combine the rice and cinnamon in enough water to cover 2 inches above the ingredients. Place in the refrigerator and let soak overnight. The following day, blend the rice, cinnamon, and sugar on high speed until finely ground. Strain through a fine colander and set aside as the concentrate. To this concentrate, you will add the milk at a 1:1 ratio. Taste will vary depending on the amount of water, so adjust the amount of milk according to your taste, but be careful not to add too much milk that you lose the flavor of the rice and cinnamon.

Cory McCollow, NIDO, Oakland

PINCHE FRESAS
ENCHANTINGLY IRREVERENT, FROZEN ENTERTAINMENT

Another one of those "leave your judgments at the door" drinks, this frozen treasure was first blended by San Antonio barman Houston Eaves for a 2014 Mezcal Vago pop-up at La Olla in Oaxaca City. "The joke about the Pinche Fresas cocktail is related to a popular style of joke-telling in Mexico about double entendres and puns. It is called *albur*," Eaves explains. "*Pinche fresas* roughly translates to 'fucking yuppies' and also 'fucking strawberries' in Spanish. So, the double meaning of this one is that the people who order frozen strawberry drinks are yuppies, and the bartender doesn't like making fruity blender drinks. So when the bartender mumbles 'Pinche fresas' under their breath while walking to the blender to make the drink, they are cursing both the drink order and the person who ordered it. But, it's boozy, flavorful, delicious, and it makes people drink mezcal and vermouth together, so the bartender can't be too mad about it."

1 OUNCE mezcal

1 OUNCE blanc vermouth

½ OUNCE fresh lemon juice

½ OUNCE simple syrup

2 STRAWBERRIES

8–10 LEAVES of *hierba buena* (mint)

MORE MINT, for garnish

Add 2 cups of pebble ice and blend all ingredients in blender. Pour into hurricane glass and garnish with strawberry and *hierba buena*.

Houston Eaves, Esquire Tavern, San Antonio

EL BURRO FANTASMA

A FIESTA-READY PUNCH, POR DOS

Everyone loves a good party, but you don't need a special occasion to bust out this killer punch. Right for any time or place, the drink was crafted in the image of barman Nacho Jimenez's favorite spicy Mexican candies, with "a bit of bitterness from both the Aperol and grapefruit blending perfectly with the smoke of the mezcal," he says. The taste is lively, but my favorite part of the drink is the garnish. Piles of bright, fresh carnations decorate the drink, echoing the way donkeys tote wagons full of flowers to holidays and other celebrations throughout the smaller, rural areas of Mexico.

3 OUNCES Pelotón de la Muerte mezcal

1 OUNCE Aperol

1 OUNCE agave

1½ OUNCES fresh grapefruit juice

1½ OUNCES fresh lime juice

4 DASHES chili tincture

FRESH CARNATIONS, for garnish

Combine the mezcal, Aperol, agave, grapefruit juice, lime juice, and chili tincture in a shaker tin with ice. Shake and strain into a punch bowl (or divide between two punch glasses) and garnish with fresh flowers. Serves two.

For the chili tincture, combine a liter of high-proof vodka (or Everclear) with 100 grams of arbol chiles and let steep for 48–72 hours, depending on the level of heat you prefer. Strain chiles out and store in a cool place.

Nacho Jimenez, Ghost Donkey, New York City

GLOSSARY

agave Plant used to make mezcal.

aguamiel Also known as "honey water," aguamiel is the liquid or sap extracted from the very center of the agave piña. It's sugary sweet, and when fermented transforms into a kombucha-like beverage called *pulque*.

añejo One of three age designations for agave spirits. For a mezcal to be labeled as *añejo*, it must be matured for at least one year in oak containers.

bacanora Mezcal from the state of Sonora cannot be called "mezcal" because it's made outside of the official Appellation of Origin. However, when mezcal is made from the *Agave angustifolia* species in the state of Sonora, it is called *bacanora*.

bagasse Agave fibers and pulp left over after cooked agave hearts have been milled or shredded. The bagasse serves many purposes, from fodder stuffed between burning hot wood and raw agaves in the pit, to use as a sealant on stills.

chapulíne Spanish word for grasshoppers. Chapulínes are often toasted and served as a bar snack alongside mezcal, or sometimes ground up and mixed with salt to make *sal de chapulínes*. Sounds gross . . . tastes delectably salty and savory.

copita Small, shallow Del Maguey Mezcal—designed terracotta drinking wares created as a nod to the traditional use of clay in mezcal distillation. Sip slowly for best results.

en barro Spanish term for "in clay." Means that the still used in mezcal production was made out of clay. Mezcal distilled in clay pots is called *mezcal en barro*.

gusano Also referred to as the *gusano del maguey*, agave worms are actually moth larvae that live in the roots and heart of the agave. If left to their own devices, they will decimate the plant from the inside out, so farmers quickly learned to harvest the bugs as a means of preservation. They're sometimes crushed and mixed with salt to create *sal de gusano*, a common accompaniment to mezcal.

horno Oven used to cook agaves. The term can be used for both underground ovens and those that sit above ground.

jícara Hollowed-out half-gourd. The most traditional vessel used for drinking mezcal.

joven Spanish word for young. Joven mezcal is made in accordance with the official rules and the correct Appellation of Origin, and hasn't been aged in any kind of wood barrel.

maestro mezcalero Master distiller in charge of all production details and decisions at a distillery.

maguey Another word for agave.

mezcaleria Bar that only sells mezcal and other agave spirits.

palenque Oaxacan term for distillery. In other states, the facilities can be called different things. For example, in Jalisco, they're called *vinatas* or *tabernas*. In Guerrero, *fábrica* is a common name.

palenquero Distillery workers, who do much of the heavy lifting at a palenque. From hacking raw agaves into chunks to filling the pits and tending to the stills, responsibilities vary by facility. This is the common term in Oaxaca.

pechuga Mezcal that has ingredients like fruit, spices, or meat added to the still between distillations.

penca Leaves or arms of the agave plant. These long, spiky offshoots are chopped off before the agave plant is cooked and transformed into mezcal.

piña The part of the agave used to make mezcal, named for its pineapple-like shape.

pulque Fermented agave sap. Often has a tangy, kombucha-like flavor.

raicilla Mezcal from the state of Jalisco cannot be called "mezcal" because it's made outside of the official Appellation of Origin. However, mezcal made there is commonly referred to as *raicilla*.

reposado Mezcal rested or aged for a minimum of two months in oak barrels can legally be considered reposado.

tahona Large stone wheel used to crush agave fibers. Tahonas are so heavy they're usually rigged to a rotating system that's propelled around in circles by a mule or donkey.

veladora Originally used as prayer candles in Catholic churches, *veladoras* are shot glass–sized glass containers (usually with a cross emblazoned on the bottom) used for drinking mezcal.

vinasses Leftover liquid from the distillation process. Vinasses are said to be toxic to the earth in large quantities and thus represent a point of concern for the industry as companies start to scale up.

ACKNOWLEDGMENTS

This book wouldn't have happened without my awesome editor, Dennis Pernu. Thanks for plucking me from the ether and giving me the freedom to write this love letter to mezcal. It was a gamble for you, and liberating for me, and I can't thank you enough for the opportunity.

On the mezcal side of things, huge thanks to the families who welcomed Zach and me into their homes in Oaxaca: Salomón Rey Rodriguez, Aquilino García López, Don Abel Lopez, Alberto Morales, Graciela Angeles Carreño, and Asis Cortés, your hospitality left a lasting impression, and I hope I do your stories justice. Big shout-out to Francisco Terrazas and Iván Saldaña Oyarzábal for letting me bug the shit out of you both with the most nitpicky details. Same goes for Camille Austin and Misty Kalkofen—you guys are the best. Alejandro Santa-Cruz and Kenny Flores, thanks for adding some fun to the mix with that amazing cemetery trip. Caitlin Laman and Arik Torren, many thanks for your candid opinions—the world needs more no-bullshit people like you.

To the bar owners, managers, and bartenders who opened their doors to let me shoot photos in your beautiful spaces, thank you! This wouldn't look nearly as good without your willingness to help: Kevin Diedrich at PCH, Kim Roselle at Trick Dog, Michael Rubel at Estereo, Aaron Pollack at the Dawson, Karla Moles and El Palenquito, Joaquín Simó at Pouring Ribbons, Courtenay Greenleaf at Masa y Agave, Silvia Philion at Mezcaloteca, Jason Cox at El Destilado, and Nacho Jimenez at Ghost Donkey.

Thanks also to: Bar Agricole, Forgery, Whisler's, the Pastry War, Half Step, Backbeat, Gracias Madre, Contigo, Licorería Limantour, Employees Only, La Condesa, Mezcaleria Las Flores, Scofflaw, GreenRiver, and Sabina Sabe.

To the mezcal brands that sent over samples for review, and some of my PR and spirit brand homies for helping out with product for recipe testing: Manuela Savona, Rachel Blom and Campari America, BC Merchants, Chiyo Takemoto and Monique Huston at Winebow, Kaj Hackinen, Ansley Coale, Mezcal Amaras, Elisandro Gonzales, Jake Lustig, Ilegal Mezcal, Danny Mena, Chris Hampson, Curt and Scott Goldman, Éva Pelczer, William Scanlin, Julio Mestre, David Suro, Yira Vallejo, Paula Gonzales, Cecilia Murrieta, and Brandon Turner with Mezcal El Silencio.

Last, but definitely not least, thanks to my family for the encouragement and support on the home front. Dad, thanks for teaching me the art of quiet fortitude and patience; Mom, for planting the seeds of writing/editing early and teaching me how to ride out the creative process; and Leif, I'm so proud of the strong and steady person you're turning into, and your support has meant the world to me. Steph and Court, for helping while I was on the road (love you, sisters), and Zach—*mi media naranja*—this book should really have a double byline for all of the work you've done to help bring it to life. You are my everything.

WHERE TO DRINK

Below is a list of some of the best places to seek out for good mezcal selections. This isn't a comprehensive list of every bar in America that serves a decent collection, but rather a relatively biased selection of places that are good to visit *specifically* for the mezcal (and sometimes mezcal cocktails), with interesting, curated lists. Don't see your city on the list? Don't worry—it's likely only a matter of time before quality agave options arrive.

LOS ESTADOS UNIDOS

CALIFORNIA
Bear vs. Bull
San Francisco, CA
2550 Mission St.
(628) 333-5754
bearvsbullbar.com

Calavera
Oakland, CA
2337 Broadway St.
(510) 338-3273
calaveraoakland.com

Cantina Mayahuel
San Diego, CA
2934 Adams Ave.
(619) 283-6292
facebook.com/
    cantinamayahuel

Comal
Berkeley, CA
2020 Shattuck Ave.
(510) 926-6300
comalberkeley.com

Gracias Madre
Los Angeles, CA
8905 Melrose Ave.
(323) 978-2170
graciasmadreweho.com

Guelaguetza
Los Angeles, CA
3014 W. Olympic Blvd.
(213) 427-0608
ilovemole.com

Las Perlas
Los Angeles, CA
107 E. 6th St.
(213) 988-8355
213nightlife.com/lasperlas

Loló
San Francisco, CA
974 Valencia St.
415-643-5656
lolosf.com

Mezcalito
San Francisco, CA
2323 Polk St.
(415) 441-2323
mezcalitosf.com

Nido
Oakland, CA
444 Oak St.
(510) 444-6436
nidooakland.com

Nopalito
San Francisco, CA
306 Broderick St.
(415) 437-0303
nopalitosf.com

COLORADO
Jimmy's
Aspen, CO
205 S. Mill St.
(970) 925-6020
jimmysaspen.com

Palenque Mezcaleria
Denver, CO
1294 S. Broadway
(303) 997-5359
palenquemezcaleria.com

FLORIDA
Sweet Liberty
Miami, FL
237-B 20th St.
(305) 763.8217
mysweetliberty.com

ILLINOIS
Big Star
Chicago, IL
1531 N. Damen Ave.
(773) 235-4039
bigstarchicago.com

Dove's Luncheonette
Chicago, IL
1545 N. Damen Ave.
(773) 645-4060
doveschicago.com

Frontera Grill
Chicago, IL
445 N. Clark St.
(312) 661-1434
rickbayless.com/
   restaurants/frontera-grill

La Mez Agave Lounge
Chicago, IL
108 W. Kinzie St.
(312) 329-9555
mercaditorestaurants.com/
   la-mez

Lena Brava
Chicago, IL
900 W. Randolph St.
(312) 733-1975
rickbayless.com/
   restaurants/lena-brava

Masa Azul
Chicago, IL
2901 W. Diversey Ave.
(773) 687-0300
masaazul.com

Mezcaleria Las Flores
Chicago, IL
3149 W. Logan Blvd.
(773) 278-2215
mezcalerialasflores.com

Presidio
Chicago, IL
1749 N. Damen Ave.
(773) 697-3315
presidiochicago.com

Quiote
Chicago, IL
2456 N. California Ave.
(312) 878-8571
quiotechicago.com

LOUISIANA
Cure
New Orleans, LA
4905 Freret St.
(504) 302-2357
curenola.com

MARYLAND
Clavel
Baltimore, MD
225 W. 23rd St.
(443) 900-8983
barclavel.com

MASSACHUSETTS
Drink
Boston, MA
348 Congress St.
(617) 695-1806
drinkfortpoint.com

Lone Star Taco Bar
Boston, MA
479 Cambridge St.
(617) 782-8226
lonestar-boston.com

NEW YORK
Casa Mezcal
New York, NY
86 Orchard St
(212) 777-2661
casamezcalny.com

Casa Neta
New York, NY
40 E. 20th St.
(212) 529-7870
casanetanyc.com

Cosme
New York, NY
35 E. 21st St.
(212) 913-9659
cosmenyc.com

Empellon
New York, NY
230 W. 4th St.
(212) 367-0999
empellon.com

El Atoradero
Brooklyn, NY
708 Washington Ave.
(718) 399-8226
elatoraderobrooklyn.com

Ghost Donkey
New York, NY
4 Bleeker St.
(212) 254-0350
ghostdonkey.com

La Biblioteca
New York, NY
622 3rd Ave.
(212) 808-8110
richardsandoval.com/
   labiblioteca

La Contenta
New York, NY
102 Norfolk St.
(212) 432-4180
lacontentanyc.com

La Loba Cantina
New York, NY
709 Church Ave.
(347) 295-1141
lalobacantina.com

Leyenda
Brooklyn, NY
221 Smith St.
(347) 987-3260
leyendabk.com

Masa y Agave
New York, NY
41 Murray St.
(212) 849-2885
rosamexicano.com/
   masayagave

Mayahuel
New York, NY
304 E. 6th St.
(212) 253-5888
Mayahuelny.com

SOUTH CAROLINA
Minero
Charleston, SC
153 E. Bay St.
(843) 789-2241
minerorestaurant.com/
   charleston

TEXAS

400 Rabbits
Austin, TX
5701 Slaughter Ln.
(512) 861-7070
400rabbitsbar.com

Bar Ilegal
Austin, TX
609 Davis St.
(512) 494-4120
clivebar.com

El Naranjo
Austin, TX
85 Rainey St.
(512) 474-2776
elnaranjorestaurant.com

Esquire Tavern
San Antonio, TX
155 E. Commerce St.
(210) 222-2521
Esquiretavern-sa.com

King Bee Lounge
Austin, TX
1906 E. 12th St.
(512) 600-6956
facebook.com/King-
    Bee-1462071510718466

La Condesa
Austin, TX
400 W. 2nd St.
(512) 499-0300
lacondesa.com

The Pastry War
Houston, TX
310 Main St.
(713) 225-3310
thepastrywar.com

Takoba
Austin, TX
1411 E. 7th St.
(512) 628-4466
takobarestaurant.com

**Techo Mezcaleria &
Agave Bar**
Austin, TX
2201 Manor Rd.
(512) 480-8441
mimadresrestaurant.com

**Whisler's & Mezcalería
Tobalá**
Austin, TX
1816 E. 6th St.
(512) 480-0781
whislersatx.com

WASHINGTON

Barrio
Seattle, WA
1420 12th Ave.
(206) 588-8105
barriorestaurant.com

Liberty Bar
Seattle, WA
517 15th Ave. E.
(206) 323-9898
libertybars.com

Mezcaleria Oaxaca
Seattle, WA
422 E. Pine St.
(206) 324-0506
mezcaleriaoaxaca.com

WASHINGTON, D.C.

Espita
Washington, D.C.
1250 9th St. NW
(202) 621-9695
espitadc.com

Oyamel
Washington, DC
401 7th St. NW
(202) 628-1005
oyamel.com

MEXICO

OAXACA

El Destilado
Oaxaca, Mexico
5 de Mayo 409
+52 951 516 2226
eldestilado.com

In Situ Mezcaleria
Oaxaca, Mexico
Calle José María
    Morelos 511
+52 951 514 1811
insitumezcaleria.com

Mezcaloteca
Oaxaca, Mexico
Reforma 506
+52 951 514 0082
mezcaloteca.com

Mezcalogia
Oaxaca, Mexico
Calle de Manuel García
    Vigil 509
+52 951 514 0115
facebook.com/mezcalogia.
    oficial

Mezcaleria Cuish
Oaxaca, Mexico
Díaz Ordaz 712
+52 951 516 8791
mezcalescuish.com/home/
    la-mezcaleria

Origen
Oaxaca, Mexico
Av. Hidalgo 820
+52 951 501 1764
origenoaxaca.com

Sabina Sabe
Oaxaca, Mexico
5 de Mayo 209
facebook.com/
    sabinasabeoaxaca

MEXICO CITY

Baltra
Mexico City, Mexico
Iztaccíhuatl 36D, Condesa
+52 55 5264 1279
baltra.bar

Bósforo
Mexico City, Mexico
Luis Moya 31, Centro
+52 55 5512 1991

El Palenquito
Mexico City, Mexico
Av. Álvaro Obregón 39,
    Roma Norte
+52 55 5207 8617
facebook.com/
    elpalenquitomezcaleria

Fifty Mils
Mexico City, Mexico
Paseo de la Reforma 500,
    Zona Rosa
+52 55 5230 1818
fourseasons.com/mexico/
    dining/lounges/fifty_mils

La Botica
Mexico City, Mexico
Multiple Locations
labotica.com.mx

La Clandestina
Mexico City, Mexico
Av. Álvaro Obregón 298,
    Condesa
+52 55 5212 1871
facebook.com/
    laclandestinamezcaleria

La Lavandería
Mexico City, Mexico
Av. Álvaro Obregón 298,
    Condesa
+52 55 5211 7142
facebook.com/
    LaLavanderiaMezcaleria

Licorería Limantour
Mexico City, Mexico
Av. Álvaro Obregón 206,
    Roma Norte
+52 55 5264 4122
limantour.tv

Maison Artemisia
Mexico City, Mexico
Tonalá 23, Colonia Roma
+52 55 6303 2471
maisonartemisia.com

Romita Comedor
Mexico City, Mexico
Av. Álvaro Obregón 49,
    Roma Norte
+52 55 5525 8975
romitacomedor.com

CANADA

El Rey
2a Kensington Ave.
Toronto, ON
elreybar.com

La Mezcaleria
1622 Commercial Dr.
Vancouver, BC
(604) 559-8226
lamezcaleria.ca

WHERE TO BUY

Alchemy Bottle Shop
alchemybottleshop.com

Astor Wines & Spirits
astorwines.com

Binny's
binnys.com

Cask
caskstore.com

Drink Up NY
drinkupny.com

K&L Wine Merchants
klwines.com

Mercado de Mezcal
mercadodemezcal.com

Mission Liquor
missionliquor.com

BIBLIOGRAPHY

Aguilera, Rodrigo. "On the Margins: Why Mexico's Southern States Have Fallen Behind." *Huffington Post*, August 10, 2015. http://www.huffingtonpost.com/rodrigo-aguilera/on-the-margins-why-mexico_b_7967874.html.

Bowen, Sarah. *Divided Spirits: Tequila, Mezcal, and the Politics of Production*. Oakland, CA: University of California Press, 2015.

Cancino, Hipócrates Nolasco. Informe 2016. Oaxaca: Consejo Regulador del Mezcal, 2016. http://www.crm.org.mx/PDF/INF_ACTIVIDADES/INFORME2015.pdf.

Conabio. "Agave: Mezcales y Diversidad." *Artes de México #98: Mezcal Arte Tradicional* (2010): Insert.

Consejo Regulador del Mezcal. "Denominación de Origen Mezcal." Last modified in 2015. http://www.crm.org.mx.

Frizell, St. John. "Mezcal: National Spirit." *Saveur*, November 11, 2009. http://www.saveur.com/article/Wine-and-Drink/National-Spirit.

Garrone, Max. "Erick Rodriguez gets what he wants." *Mezcalistas*, February 3, 2015. http://mezcalistas.com/erick-rodriguez-gets-what-he-wants.

Heugel, Bobby. "Chasing Mezcal in One of Mexico's Most Dangerous Regions." *Punch*, June 26, 2014. http://punchdrink.com/articles/chasing-mezcal-in-one-of-mexicos-most-dangerous-regions.

Heugel, Bobby. "Understanding Mezcal and its Amazing Ascent." *Eater*, June 5, 2015. http://www.eater.com/spirits/2015/6/5/8734643/understanding-mezcal-and-its-amazing-ascent.

Mexicana Secretaría de Comercio y Fomento Industrial, NOM-070-SCFI-1994, Mexico City: Diario Oficial de la Federación, 1994. http://www.dof.gob.mx/nota_detalle. php?codigo=4883475 &fecha=12/06/1997.

Saldaña Oyarzábal, Iván. *The Anatomy of Mezcal*. Milton, DE: Expresslt Media, 2016.

Saltzstein, Dan. "Hoping Mezcal Can Turn the Worm." *New York Times*, April 21, 2009. http://www.nytimes.com/2009/04/22/dining/22mezcal.html.

Martineau, Chantal. *How The Gringos Stole Tequila: The Modern Age of México's Most Traditional Spirit*. Chicago, IL: Chicago Review Press, 2015.

Mendoza, Dr. Abisaí Josué García. "A Geography of Mezcal." *Artes de México #98: Mezcal Arte Tradicional* (2010): 82–83.

Rasero, Fausto. "Of Wisdom and Eternity." *Artes de México #98: Mezcal Arte Tradicional* (2010): 92–93.

Sánchez, Santiago Ruy. "Along the Roads of Oaxacan Mezcal." *Artes de México #98: Mezcal Arte Tradicional* (2010): 88–91.

Terrazas, Francisco. "Fermentation." *Mas Mezcal*, February 12, 2016. http://www.masmezcal.com/mezcalvago/fermentation

The Pastry War. "Captain's List." Last modified August 2, 2016. http://www.thepastrywar.com.

Torrentera, Ulises. *Mezcalaria: Cultura del Mezcal*, 3rd ed. Oaxaca, Mexico: Farolito Ediciones, 2012.

Young, Naren. "Naked & Famous Mezcal Cocktail Recipe." *Food Republic*, August 16, 2011. http://www.foodrepublic.com/recipes/naked-famous-mezcal-cocktail-recipe.

INDEX

ABOUT THE AUTHOR

EMMA JANZEN is a journalist and photographer specializing in all things cocktails, spirits, and design. Currently the digital content editor for *Imbibe* magazine, her work has appeared in *Punch*, *Bon Appétit*, *Food Republic*, and *Dwell*. She lives in Chicago with her husband and two tuxedo cats.